All about the
Lhasa Apso

All about the Lhasa Apso

Juliette Cunliffe

PELHAM BOOKS
STEPHEN GREENE PRESS

Dedicated to the memory of Di Trudgill,
in recollection of her much valued friendship

PELHAM BOOKS/STEPHEN GREENE PRESS

Published by the Penguin Group
27 Wrights Lane, London W8 5TZ, England
Viking Penguin Inc., 40 West 23rd Street, New York, New York 10010, USA
The Stephen Greene Press, 15 Muzzey Street, Lexington, Massachusetts 02173, USA

Penguin Books Australia Ltd, Ringwood, Victoria, Australia
Penguin Books Canada Ltd, 2801 John Street, Markham, Ontario, Canada L3R 1B4
Penguin Books (NZ) Ltd, 182–190 Wairau Road, Auckland 10, New Zealand

Penguin Books Ltd, Registered Offices: Harmondsworth, Middlesex, England

First published 1990

Copyright © 1990 by Juliette Cunliffe

Made and printed in Great Britain
Typeset in Plantin by Butler & Tanner Ltd, Frome and London

A CIP catalogue record for this book is available from the British Library.
ISBN 0 7207 1880

Contents

Foreword

by Lady Freda Valentine CBE,
President of the Lhasa Apso Club

This is a book for which we have waited for some time and at last we have the pleasure of knowing that it is now on the market. I wish it every success and would like to say how very clearly and succinctly it has been put together.

Due to the author's clearness and her grasp of the subject, I hope this book will help a great many people in their efforts to continue to improve the breed and to solve any problems they may encounter.

AUTHOR'S NOTE: Sadly Lady Freda Valentine passed away on 10 January, 1989 whilst this book was in the process of publication. She had reached the great age of ninety-three years.

Credits

The author and publishers are grateful to the following for permission to reproduce copyright photographs: Malcolm Baird page 47; Juliette Cunliffe page 125; Richard Davies page 106; Thomas Fall pages 8, 28, 46 (right), 50; Andrew Frankl page 48 (left); Dave Freeman pages 45 (bottom right), 81; Gloucestershire Newspapers page 101; Mr Hartley page 53; Mrs Hesketh-Williams page 45 (top left): Diane Pearce pages 9, 11, 42, 43, 45 (top right), 48 (right), 49, 51 (bottom), 109; Rob Richardson pages 44, 45 (centre left), 45 (centre right), 46 (left), 51 (top), 75, 91, 97, 105 (top); Anne Rolin-Williams page 45 (bottom left); Kresten Scheel page 52; *Sevenoaks Chronicle* page 30; Sport and General pages 34, 104; Sally-Anne Thompson page 10. Every effort has been made to trace copyright owners but in some cases this has not been possible.

The Breed Standard is reproduced by permission of the Kennel Club.

Preface

It is my hope that the following pages contain much of interest both to new and prospective Lhasa Apso owners and to experienced enthusiasts of the breed. It is difficult to strike a happy balance but I hope that readers will feel that I have done so as far as is possible.

One of the most heartening things about carrying out research for a breed book is that so many people seem glad to pass on their knowledge, often acquired over many years, so that it may be committed to paper for the sake of posterity.

To Lady Freda Valentine I extend a very warm 'Thank you' for so graciously consenting to write a short foreword and for her much valued interest. Her treasured 'damask pink book', containing a medley of news-clippings, show catalogues, and photographs from the early 1930s onwards, has provided me with much information, some of which I have been able to pass on in the pages which follow.

To Ann Wynyard I owe my very special thanks for so generously allowing me to borrow much of her own personal research material. Her trust has been greatly appreciated and I feel sure that the content of this book has been enriched by her kind gesture.

It is thanks to Clifford Hubbard that I have discovered much of the information which I have included about the breed in India. His own personal library is like an Aladdin's cave and I am more than grateful to him for allowing me to share its contents.

I should also like to express my appreciation to Daphne Hesketh-Williams for the loan of her early newsletters, to Stanley and Miriam Chandler for the literature they have provided, to the Kennel Club and its library staff for allowing me to use their library facilities and last, but by no means least, to my long-suffering partner in dogs, Carol Johnson, who has patiently proof-read and listened to countless hours of noisy word-processing.

Without writing a 'Who's Who' in the world of Apsos it is not possible to pay tribute here to everyone I would like, but I do, very sincerely, wish to thank all those who have shown interest and who have offered or provided photographic material and information.

The frustrating thing about having, sooner or later, to finish writing a book of this nature is that one has acquired so much material that it is simply not possible to include everything. My interest over a number of years has led me to accumulate an enormous amount of information, not only about Lhasa Apsos but also about Tibet and its inhabitants, both canine and human. I know that my appetite is not yet satiated and that I shall continue my search to uncover hitherto 'forgotten' material for many years to come!

Juliette P. A. Cunliffe

1 History and Habitat in Tibet

Whilst there are claims that the Lhasa Apso has been in existence since 800 BC we must bear in mind that the earliest written records of Tibet did not come into being until around AD 639. Thus it is very difficult to substantiate such claims, although it is highly likely that the Lhasa Apso did indeed exist prior to the birth of Christ.

The breed possibly descended originally from European and Asiatic herding dogs such as the Puli and the Pumi; undoubtedly the Apso has lived, relatively unchanged, in the monasteries and homes of Tibetan nobles for many centuries. Clearly, though, it was not kept exclusively in monasteries as has sometimes been stated.

These little, shaggy-coated Tibetan dogs were, however, considered a talisman and were not sold but given only as gifts. From the beginning of the Manchu Dynasty in 1583 until 1908, the end of Dowager Empress Tsu Hsi's reign, the Dalai Lama (for, as a reincarnation, there is only one) had a custom of presenting these dogs to the imperial families of China as bringers of good fortune.

The history of the breed is veiled in a certain haze but it seems that some, at least, were bred and selected with care, being jealously guarded by the Buddhist monks. It is perhaps a little-known fact that when the 14th Dalai Lama was young he had a black Lhasa Apso 'of which he was very fond'.[1] We know, too, that the breed has always been held in high esteem, although there is no firm evidence to suggest that it holds any religious significance. It is interesting to note that even recent travellers to Tibet make mention of little dogs peeping out from the folds of the Tibetan Buddhists' robes. One of the reasons why it has been so difficult to establish the breed outside Tibet is that the majority of typical specimens were confined to the monasteries or owned by the nobles who, like the Lamaist monks, were seldom willing to part with them.

It does seem, however, that not all lived a life of luxury in Tibet for in James Watson's *The Dog Book*, which was published in 1906, we learn that one of the imports of that era was 'purchased out of a Bhuteer's market cart'. He tells us that the dog was 'unkempt, unwashed, uninviting, and loath to be civilised', and that 'he valiantly

Tibetan peasant with his two Apsos.

guarded his vegetables, till made reluctantly to understand that he was born for higher things and that a show career beyond the waters awaited him'. We are told, too, that the dog in question was quite prepared to protect his goods and chattels to grim death and that he was by no means friendly, though he had devoted himself to one owner for years. This description must not, however, detract from the fact that he, too, must surely have been held in high esteem, for his function in life was clearly a very important one. This dog was, in fact, Kepwick Tuko, and he apparently had to be very carefully guarded whilst in Tibet or he would promptly have disappeared, for we are told that the 'wily Asiatic' was 'fully aware of the value of really good specimens'.

But by no means all came from market carts for, on the other hand, we hear of one Apso who eventually came to England having been brought from the interior of Tibet, 'accompanied by an attendant wreathed in Turquoises', and another we know of was carried across the saddle for miles and miles. Indeed this enchanting little breed of ours certainly captured many a fond heart in his home country too.

Theories on the Origin of the Name of our Breed

Theories put forward regarding the name of the breed are varied, and although I have reason to doubt the correctness of some of the theories, I am not in a position to oppose them with confidence unless I have proof. I have, however, had several discussions with Tibetans in an effort to find out more about the Lhasa Apso and about the origin of its name. Perhaps the most honest approach is to put forward all the theories so that the reader may attempt to draw his own conclusions.

There is no doubt in my mind that 'Apso' would be more correct than Lhasa Apso for it is certain that Tibetans refer to our little fellow simply as 'Apso'. It is we foreigners who have introduced the word Lhasa, for that is where we believed the best specimens were to be found. Indeed it is true to say that the word 'Apso' can be used to mean any long-coated dog but I am assured by Tibetans themselves

Lhassa Terrier – 'Tuko'.

that 'Apso' is used primarily with reference to the short-legged, long-coated dog. Those to whom I spoke were well aware of the difference between the Tibetan Terrier and the Lhasa Apso and it was the latter to which they were referring. This is borne out by a number of early Indian writers too.

It has been said time and time again that 'Apso' is a derivation of the word 'Rapso' which supposedly means 'goat-like' (Tibetan goats are small and long-coated). However, the Tibetans to whom I have suggested this have laughed openly and have suggested that foreigners like to look for connections which are often entirely without foundation. They are adamant that even the academics can be wrong and feel that the same inaccuracy has been copied many times over. 'Rapso' seems not to be a Tibetan word at all, the word for goat being 'ra', but certainly 'Apso' does conjure up a picture of something shaggy coated. The term 'Apso' (or 'Apsok' as the Tibetans say) means 'long-haired'.

I suspect that Mr J. Taring's explanation[2] is probably as accurate as we shall find: 'Apso is short for Ara – moustache and sog-sog – hairy. So, the name apso means hairy moustache.'

Sometimes we have heard that the breed was known as 'Apso (or Abso) Seng Kyi', or 'Bark Sentinel Lion Dog'. Indeed 'kyi' means dog and 'seng' means lion, but I have yet to fathom out quite how 'bark sentinel' has crept in, although one Tibetan did say that 'ab' represents the noise of barking. By my reckoning 'hairy moustached lion dog' seems more accurate and equally appropriate. But to take our reasoning a stage further, if 'ab' indicates barking and so(k) means 'hairy', have we perhaps a 'barking, hairy lion dog'? Or are we doing just what the Tibetans say we shouldn't do in looking for an explanation?

Undoubtedly the lion is an animal of great significance throughout the Buddhist world although there are, in fact, no lions in Tibet; indeed even the Dalai Lama's throne at Lhasa is supported by carved lions. They were legendary creatures and often the Lord Buddha and other deities were depicted riding a lion which could be turned into a small likeness at will. As legend progressed, the lion became a small type of dog which could be transformed by Buddha into a fierce lion when he needed defence against the enemy. A fascinating 'gem' in relation to the myth which surrounds the lion is the legend which was invented to explain the lion's twisted curls – 'Buddha remained so long in motionless contemplation that the snails crawled over his head.'[1] Another Lamaist theory is that there were five large curls on the lion's head 'to simulate the flags worn in the ancient head-dress of high military officials'.[1] Indeed, one cannot help but seek some connection between our beloved little Tibetan 'lion dog' and the Kylin, found in so many forms throughout Tibet and the Far East. We shall come to the Breed Standard later but I find it sad that the 'dense mane' was written out of the most recent Kennel Club Standard for I feel sure that this was significant.

It is perhaps interesting to note that Mukandi Lal tells us that 'some students of Chinese history are of the opinion that carvings and statues of "lions" in China are really the images of this wonderful breed, which looks like a lion and has a mane like a lion's'[1].

Just to clarify the word 'Abso', this has no literal meaning in the Tibetan language but is a Mongolian word. With reference to Mongolia, Rahul Sankrityan, an Indian scholar of the Tibetan language and someone who lived in Lhasa and the monasteries of Tibet, is of the opinion that the breed may in fact be of Mongolian origin for, in the Mongolian language, 'Apso' means 'wholly-covered – with hair all over'.

The fact that the Tibetans wrote no books about their dogs does not help us in our understanding of the origin of the name but, if we are to begin to understand these charming little dogs themselves, let us now take a closer look at the environment in Tibet.

Environment

Tibet conjures up pictures of Himalayan mountains covered in snow but, in fact, it is a land full of variety. Tibet is actually in the Himalayan rain shadow and in consequence is quite dry and sunny throughout the year. Heavy snowfalls are far less common than one would imagine and, despite little rain, flooding can be a serious problem, for the sun is quick to melt the snows.

A high table land, with the plains around Lhasa about 2 miles (3.2 km) above sea level, Tibet is equivalent to Great Britain, France and Germany in area and suffers extremes of temperature. From early morning to midday the temperature may vary from below zero to 38 °C (below 32 °F to 100 °F). In the north and west of the country it can drop to −40 °C (−40 °F) and there are fewer than a hundred days in each year which are free from frost. Northern monsoons can sweep across the plains for several days, bringing with them duststorms, sandstorms, snowstorms and, on occasion, rainstorms.

Weather conditions are therefore extremely rough and this, doubtless, is one of the reasons why the Lhasa Apso is such a hardy little breed. We would do well to consider also that the altitude of the country creates a very rarefied air and, like the peoples of its homeland, the Apso needs good strong lungs if is to survive successfully in the environment to which it was originally accustomed.

Before we move on to the dogs themselves it is highly relevant to

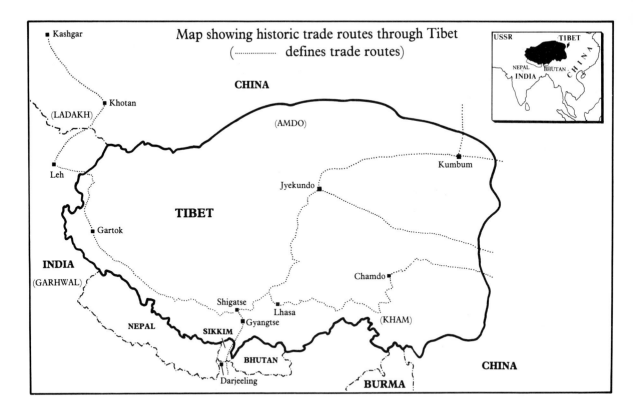

Map showing historic trade routes through Tibet
(............... defines trade routes)

take a brief look at the Tibetan people and their culture. Tibet has always been a land steeped in religion, Tibetan Buddhism, which succeeded the shamanistic Bon religion of the country, having permeated every aspect of Tibetan life. Virtually all Tibetan literature and art is religious and, until the Chinese took over, between a quarter and a third of the male population were monks. Indeed until 1950 the political and social structure also had remained virtually unchanged for several centuries, amongst lay people the primary division being between the aristocratic landowners and the peasants who owed them service in return for land. In such a vast country there were, of course, also the nomads and the traders.

But let us go back for a moment to the religion of Tibet, for it does indeed have a bearing on the subject of this book. The ruler of Tibet is the Dalai Lama who is chosen by the principle of reincarnation. When a Dalai Lama dies his reincarnation is sought out, and chosen to succeed him is a child who has been identified by a number of signs. It is the reincarnation theory which is of particular interest to us here for Buddhists believe that upon death (unless one has reached the ideal state of Nirvana) one is reborn, not necessarily as a human, in fact reincarnation on the human plane is infrequent. We may return as virtually any living being and thus it is that dogs, along with all living creatures, are treated with kindness. The Buddhist does not know whether or not the animal he meets has been known to him, or even perhaps is related to him, in this or a previous life.

Added to this, the Buddhist doctrine teaches that one's lot in a future life is determined by meritorious acts in the present and to take the life of a living creature is to commit a great sin. Indeed the fundamental principle of Buddhist ethics is that of compassion, and I believe that one of the difficulties in understanding the importance of religion in Tibet is to comprehend how great a part religion plays in the life of the layman as well as in the lives of those belonging to a monastic order.

But this is not a book about religion, it is about the Lhasa Apso. Suffice it to say that 'A well cared-for dog is considered even more fortunate than many human beings. There is a saying that though the life of a dog is the result of bad karma in its previous life, the good time that it enjoys keeps it from committing sins in this one.'[3]

Putting the Apso in Perspective

There are now four Tibetan breeds known widely in the Western world: the Tibetan Mastiff, the Tibetan Spaniel, the Tibetan Terrier, and the Lhasa Apso. A close cousin of the Apso is the Shih Tzu of China. In 1929 it was claimed that in the general Himalayan region there were no fewer than eleven[4] Tibetan breeds but, sadly, the four we now know are the only ones established outside their country of origin.

The Tibetans were indifferent about the naming of their breeds and if one were to ask a Tibetan to which breed his dog belonged he would probably answer, 'Just a dog'.

It would be difficult indeed to confuse the Lhasa Apso with the **Tibetan Mastiff** but it is probable, indeed likely, that both had common ancestors. The Mastiff is a large and powerful dog, weighing in the region of 100–140 lbs (45–63 kg) and standing 24–26 ins (60–66 cm) at the shoulder. The most usual colour of this breed in Tibet was black and tan, although red ones were not infrequently seen and those which were all black in colour were highly prized.

The Mastiff was and still is used in Tibet to guard flocks from the incursions of Tibetan beasts of prey such as the wolf, jackal, fox and snow-leopard. It was invariably chained beside tents and houses as a guard against all kinds of intruder, including unwelcome humans, and was trained from a very young age to be ferocious. Despite this the

Tibetan Mastiff. This photograph, taken in 1934, is of Drenjong Dakpa who was imported to England by the Hon. Mrs Irma Bailey.

breed is biddable and affectionate with people it knows. The name, Mastiff, in Tibet is 'Do Kyi', meaning 'dog you can tie up'.

Now, once again becoming more firmly established in England, the Tibetan Mastiff is steadily securing its place in the show ring and has proved itself to be a most pleasant companion and devoted family dog; he does not, however, lend himself to indiscriminate friendships with strangers.

The **Tibetan Spaniel**, too has been relatively clearly defined as a separate breed since the first were imported to the UK late in the nineteenth century. The coat is considerably shorter than that of the Apso and is smooth on the face and on the front of the legs. Like the Apso it has an undercoat, albeit of a different density, but the top coat is silky, a texture clearly not called for in the Lhasa Apso.

Although the overall size and balance of the two breeds are somewhat similar there are many subtle differences. There is a marked difference in forehand construction with the Spaniel's legs being 'slightly bowed'; notably the shape of the skull differs too, that of the Tibetan Spaniel being slightly domed. It is important also to note that the 'harefoot', so characteristic of the Spaniel, contrasts considerably with the 'cat-like' foot of the Apso.

Tibetan Spaniel. Ch Nan-Kyi Pooh of Braeduke, bred by Miss H. F. J. Forbes and Mrs E. J. B. Wynyard and owned by the latter. 'Nanki', sire of three champions, was *Dog World*'s and Pedigree Petfood's top winning Tibetan Spaniel in 1985 and in 1987. He won 13 Challenge Certificates with Best of Breed on 12 occasions and was Reserve in the Utility Group at the Three Counties Championship Show.

The **Tibetan Terrier** as we know it now is clearly distinguishable from the Lhasa Apso. Briefly, it is substantially longer in the leg, standing 14–16 ins (35–40 cm) at the shoulder; its foreface, too, is longer than that of the Apso and a scissor bite is called for in the breed. The Tibetan Terrier's coat, whilst long, is not as long as that of the Apso and this difference is accentuated due to the difference in height between the two breeds. Of course it differs in many other features also but those mentioned are very obviously visible, even to the untrained eye.

Confusion in the Early Years

According to Colonel Duncan, author of the famous little book, *Tomu From Tibet*, the earliest Apso we know of in England was brought here in 1854 but, although the Tibetan Terrier and the Lhasa Apso are now well defined, that has not always been the case. Indeed there has been a tremendous amount of confusion over the years. At the turn of this century the dogs we now know as Lhasa Apsos and Tibetan Terriers were known variously as Thibetan, Bhutan, Bhuteer or Lhassa Terriers and in 1901 Mr Lionel Jacob, a government official in the Punjab and

Tibetan Terrier. Ch Amdos of Antartica, bred and owned by Mr and Mrs K. B. Rawlings, is the holder of a record number of 42 Challenge Certificates as well as Group and Best in Show awards. Son of an almost equally famous dam, who was awarded 35 CCs, he was one of a litter of five puppies, four of which were destined to become champions.

organiser of the Northern Indian Kennel Club told us some were as large as 'Russian poodles' and others as small as Maltese.

Classified as one breed, even in 1900 enthusiasts were clearly aware that there were contrary types. All the Tibetan dogs had in common the fact that the tail curled strongly over the back but some were described as resembling Skye Terriers while others were 'puggy and short in face, undershot'[5] and 'with more affinity to the Japanese Spaniel'.[5]

Certainly there was a difference in both overall size and in coat. The Hon. Mrs McLaren-Morrison, of whom we shall read more later, wrote, shortly before 1904, that she would like to see much more attention paid to size for she felt that the Tibetans attached great importance to this aspect. She believed that there should be two classes, over and under a certain weight, although she did not specify what that dividing weight should be. Most authorities at that time, however, described the weight range for the 'breed' as only 8–15 lbs (roughly 4–7 kg).

In 1908 the breed had Championship status and was shown in two sizes in different classes and Miss Wild, breeder of the famous Cotsvale Lhasa Apsos, said she saw many 'beautiful and true-to-type specimens at pre-1914 shows'.[6] By this she was referring to Apsos.

However, during the troublesome years of the First World War the Lhassa Terrier struggled to survive and little was heard of it until 1929 when the 'breed' was exhibited once again. There was still great confusion, although it was quite clear from the comments of people exhibiting at the time that there were quite obviously two types of dog being shown, still as the same breed. The Hon. Mrs Irma Bailey, who spent some time in Tibet and went to some trouble to find out the kind of dog which was generally preferred, stated quite categorically that 'the long-legged dogs shown in this country would not be admired in Tibet'.[7]

The Shih Tzu Makes its Mark in Britain

As the twenties moved into the thirties there was increasing interest in the 'breed', new blood having been introduced by the Hon. Mrs Bailey who imported dogs to the UK in 1928. Confusion, however, was brought to a further peak by some dogs imported from China in 1930 by Miss Hutchins. Two of these were owned by General and Mrs Brownrigg (later to become Sir Douglas and Lady Brownrigg) and were called Tibetan Lion Dogs, this being the name most frequently

Shih Tzu. Ch Darralls Felicity was bred and owned by Mrs D. Gurney. Felicity won 8 Challenge Certificates and was top winning Shih Tzu of 1980, after which she was retired from the show ring at the age of only three years.

used in China. In the knowledge that Lhassa Terriers had been given as gifts to distinguished people in China, the dogs she imported were at first thought to be Lhassa Terriers (by this time now referred to by some sources as Lhasa Apsos).

Lady Brownrigg did not herself return to England until 1931, following which her dogs were carefully compared with the Baileys' recent imports from Tibet. The latter were found to have narrower heads, longer noses and smaller eyes than Lady Brownrigg's dogs. Nevertheless, they joined the ranks of the others and were shown alongside the Lhassa Terriers/Lhasa Apsos at the West of England Ladies' Kennel Society Championship Show in 1933. Later they were to be classified as Shih Tzus.

The Breeds Divide

In 1934 the Tibetan Breeds Association was established with the aim of drawing a distinction between the various dogs of Tibet. Indeed it was Mr A. Croxton-Smith, Chairman of the Kennel Club, who had approached Col. and Mrs Bailey and had asked them to sort out the confusion.

A meeting took place at Lady Freda Valentine's house in Green Street, London, and 'ideals' were set down. Four Tibetan breeds were officially accepted: the Lhasa Apso, the Tibetan Terrier, the Mastiff, and the Tibetan Spaniel. The Chinese dogs were named Shih Tzu and were classified separately as a breed. (It is perhaps relevant to bear in mind that until that time breeds in China had also been confused but, in 1934, the Peking Kennel Club was formed and Chinese standards were eventually drawn up in 1938.)

The following is the original Lhasa Apso Standard issued by the Tibetan Breeds Association in 1934:

'(In judging these dogs, breed characteristics are of paramount importance)

1. *Character* – Gay and assertive, but chary of strangers.

2. *Size* – Variable, but about 10 inches [25 cm] or 11 inches [28 cm] at shoulder for dogs, bitches slightly smaller.

3. *Colour* – Golden, sandy, honey, dark grizzle, slate, smoke, particolour, black, white or brown. This being the true Tibetan Lion-dog, golden or lion-like colours are preferred. Other colours in order as above. Dark tips to ears and beard are an asset.

4. *Body Shape* – The length from point of shoulders to point of buttocks

longer than height at withers, well ribbed up, strong loin, well-developed quarters and thighs.

5. *Coat* – Heavy, straight, hard, not woolly or silky, of good length and very dense.

6. *Mouth and Muzzle* – Mouth level, otherwise slightly undershot preferable. Muzzle of medium length; a square muzzle is objectionable.

7. *Head* – Heavy head furnishings with good fall over eyes, good whiskers and beard; skull narrow, falling away behind the eyes in a marked degree, not quite flat but not domed or apple-shaped; straight foreface of fair length. Nose black, about $1\frac{1}{2}$ inches [38 mm] long, or the length from tip of nose to eye to be roughly about one-third of the total length from nose to back of skull.

8. *Eyes* – Dark brown, neither very large and full, nor very small and sunk.

9. *Ears* – Pendant, heavily feathered.

10. *Legs* – Forelegs straight; both fore and hind legs heavily furnished with hair.

11. *Feet* – Well feathered, should be round and cat-like with good pads.

12. *Tail and Carriage* – Well feathered, should be carried well over back in a screw; there may be a kink at the end. A low carriage of stern is a serious fault.'

The divisions now made, we see how few Apsos there were at this time by the very fact that at Cruft's in 1935 there were only twelve Apsos entered, making nineteen entries and in the same year fourteen were exhibited at the Ladies' Kennel Association.

Some Interesting Theories from India

Mukhandi Lal, who, incidentally, was a barrister and had obtained his BA from Oxford, had exceptional opportunities to keep and to study Tibetan dogs. Born shortly before the close of the nineteenth century, and living in Garhwal in the Himalayas adjoining Tibet, he had seen and lived with Tibetan dogs since childhood. The breeds he owned at various times were Tibetan Mastiffs, Tibetan Bhoteas, Tibetan Terriers and Lhassa Terriers, 'alias Lhassa Apsos'. Luckily for Apso enthusiasts, Mr Lal felt that his knowledge of the latter was greater than that of the other breeds and he imparted a great deal of information in his informative article in *The Indian Kennel Gazette* of December

1957. Indeed Mr Lal felt that he knew the Lhasa Apso well enough to lay down 'an exact standard of points', which we shall come to a little later.

Mr Lal doubts 'if any other breed of dog has been bred to type for so many centuries continuously' and tells us that the Apso occupied a 'high place in Tibetan dogdom' and was a great favourite with the Tibetans. He clarifies that they were kept as guards and pets inside the houses of the Tibetan aristocrats, high officials and abbots of monasteries and is of the opinion that 'the purity and continuity of the breed is due to its indoor, exclusive, aristocratic behaviour'. Mr Lal considers it to be 'the most exclusive and aristocratic dog in Tibet' and tells his readers, just as so many others have done, how difficult it was to get really good specimens out of Tibet itself. Clearly he felt that most typical specimens were only to be seen in Lhasa, further than the Gharwali tradesmen ventured. Most of the Apsos in India went via Sikkim, Bhutan and Nepal, all of which are on the borders of Tibet and in which countries the inhabitants freely intermarry with the Tibetans. There was regular trade between these countries and Tibet and many Nepali merchants married and settled in Lhasa where they enjoyed special privileges.

In Mr Lal's description of the breed he tells us that the Apso is a 'clean dog', 'a loving pet' and that 'it responds to and appreciates friendly treatment and petting', being 'ever ready to respond to its owner. It differentiates between strangers and friends quickly. It is obedient. It does not like to walk on wet grass.' How terribly true I find this last statement! Mr Lal tells his readers how well the breed thrives in India's hot climate and draws our attention to Col. Duncan's comments about his bitch Tomu who had also adjusted to a variety of climates when travelling through a number of countries on her way back to England.

Mr Lal was certainly not in favour of particolours. He had very strong views on the subject and stated without hesitation that in his opinion the breed should be of 'single colour'. 'It is time that multi-colour Apsos were eliminated.'[1] Mr Lal goes on to say that in his opinion 'the following colours should be recognised in order of preference – white, black, golden, lemon, grey and red'.[1] How very interesting it is to compare Mr Lal's opinions concerning colour with those set down by Britain's team of enthusiasts in 1934 – no wonder we now specify no colour preference!

In the 'Standard of Points' set down by Mr Lal he gives points for the various sections: he issues 10 points each for head, coat and body, and 5 points for each of the other sections of his provisional 'standard'. Interestingly he required the muzzle to be short and square and 2–

3 ins (5–7.5 cm) long; coat length he specified as 3–6 ins (7.5–15 cm); weight 10–16 lbs (4.5–7 kg); with a height range 10–14 ins (25–35 cm). This latter is especially interesting for Mr Lal assures us that he was well familiar also with the Tibetan Terrier. This being the case we must assume that he was not confusing the two when he wrote his 'standard'.

The Apso Leaves Tibet

As we mentioned earlier, the Apso was never sold but was given only as a gift, making it doubly difficult for the early pioneers of the breed to obtain their foundation stock.

Miss Marjorie Wild had her first Lhassa Terrier in 1901 (or possibly 1900, for she herself reports both dates in her letters). The parents of this dog, a male, were brought back from the hills of India by Mr McLaren-Morrison. Indeed there were several reports and descriptions of Lhasa Terriers (and similar) in India from 1895. Mr McLaren-Morrison subsequently joined Sir Francis Younghusband's expedition to Tibet in 1904 following which, Miss Wild tells us, other dogs were brought back to England from Tibet.

In her own personal notes about the breed, Miss Wild described the

'Lhasa' owned by Miss Marjorie Wild. This photograph was taken in 1906. Lhasa lived to be eighteen years old.

Apsos of that era as being 'mostly blue-black and white, all black or grizzle in colour' and tells us that they were 'altogether larger and coarser than the smaller variety (called the golden Apso) which were brought over here by Col. and Hon. Mrs Eric Bailey in 1928'. Indeed all sources of reference around the turn of the century tell us primarily of varying shades of grey, black and white and it seems clear that gold was not seen in this country until Mrs Bailey's imports several years later.

Indeed, Mrs Bailey, whose husband took over from Sir Charles Bell as political officer for Tibet in 1921, went to considerable trouble to seek out the type of dogs generally preferred by the Tibetans. Her enquiries were made as a result of her close contact with many of the Tibetan nobles and she found that apart from being a small dog 'it must, as the name implies, have long hair, the longer the better within reason. Then, as regards colour, the commonest is black or iron grey, but the Tibetans prefer a golden or honey-coloured dog.'[7]

Mrs Bailey acquired her first two dogs, named Sengtru and Apso, whilst living in Sikkim on the Tibetan frontier. These had originally been given to Col. R. S. Kennedy (medical officer with Sir Charles Bell) by Tsarong Shape who was commander-in-chief. He had wished to show his gratitude for the treatment of his wife by giving a valuable present. When Col. Kennedy retired from government service in 1922 he presented the two dogs to Mrs Bailey.

Each time Mrs Bailey and her husband went to Tibet, which they did annually for seven years, they took their two dogs with them and tried hard to obtain more of the same kind.

Seemingly they could quite easily find similar dogs but they wanted 'the same type in all particulars, including especially colour'. However, they found this quite impossible until, in 1924, Col. Bailey spent a month in Lhasa and was in frequent contact with the Dalai Lama. Through His Holiness and other high officials he continued the search and eventually found a black bitch, then named Apso, which belonged to a young Tibetan officer.

The officer would not agree to part with his bitch but did allow Col. Bailey to take her away to breed from. Until then the Baileys had only bred from their original pair so new blood was essential at this stage of the development of their strain. The Baileys renamed their newly acquired bitch Demon and mated her to their dog Sengtru, resulting in the hoped-for litter. Demon was then sent back to Tibet but, sadly, she was lost on the road *en route* and was never seen again.

Col. and Mrs Bailey continued to search for more dogs to add to their stock, wishing to bring in the much needed new bloodlines but they had no further success in finding a dog which entirely matched up to their pre-determined requirements. However, shortly before their departure in 1928 they obtained Lhasa, a male, which met the requirements as nearly as possible – he was 'what we were looking for in all except colour'. Lhasa was grey and white and had belonged to Mr Martin of the British Trade Agency at Gyantse, with whom he had lived for eight years before being presented to Mrs Bailey.

The Baileys brought six Apsos back to England in 1928. These were Lhasa and five descendants of their original pair (Sengtru and Apso): Taktru, Droma, Tsitru, Pema and Litsi. When mated to golds, Lhasa, by the way, presumably produced a high proportion of gold puppies, for in 1934 Mrs Bailey wrote, 'I am glad to say that his progeny have so far been of excellent colour!' [7]

Observations made by Mrs Bailey during her long search were that the Lhassa Terriers in the interior of Tibet and near the Indian border had narrower skulls and longer muzzles, being generally more terrier-like than the Apsos found in the monasteries near the Chinese border; here they generally had shorter legs and shorter muzzles and were rather more round in eye.

The Lhasa Apso Arrives in America

Early in 1933 (the first month of the Water Bird Year to be precise) Mr and Mrs Suydam Cutting, who had seen the Baileys' Apsos in Nepal, were given two Lhasa Apsos by His Holiness the 13th Dalai Lama. This was a result of a sort of 'correspondence friendship' which had been built up between Mr Cutting and His Holiness and had, in 1931, led to Mr Cutting sending the latter presents of two Dalmatians and two 'German hounds'. A further pair of golden Apsos were sent to the Cuttings after His Holiness's death and yet another pair arrived in 1950 from the 14th Dalai Lama. Both of the latter, named Le and Phema, became American champions. Unfortunately Phema did not have puppies but Le sired several litters. It was largely through the efforts of Mr and Mrs Cutting that the Apso found its place in the American show scene and their Hamilton Kennels became known throughout the world.

Again the difficulty of obtaining stock from Tibet is reinforced when Lady Freda Valentine recalls how Mrs Cutting, upon asking if she might buy a certain Lhasa Apso that she had admired, received the response, 'You ask me to sell my child?' Others who played an important part in the history of the breed in the USA were the Lloyds of New Jersey and Miss Daisy Frazier with her Lost Horizon Kennels in California.

An Apso was exhibited (as a Lhassa Terrier) at the Westminster KC

Show in New York in 1934 and an American Standard was drawn up for the breed in 1935. This was very similar to the English Standard which had come into effect the year before.

Unfortunately there was, however, a great deal of confusion in these early years in the USA for between 1937 and 1950 some dogs were imported and registered, in good faith, as Lhasa Apsos. It later transpired that they were, in fact, Shih Tzus but by the time their true identity had been discovered they had already been bred from. As a result of this the Shih Tzu forms one of the bloodlines behind the American Lhasa Apso.

We should perhaps bear in mind that at that time the various small, long-coated breeds were confused not only in the USA but also in China and India and, indeed, they had only just about been sorted out in the UK. In the early 1930s similar types of dog were exhibited at the Peking Kennel Club as Lhassa Poodles, Lhassa Lion Dogs and Lhassa Terriers, to name but a few!

If one traces back very carefully it is perfectly possible to see where the 'crosses' were made in America and, as a result, to calculate the proportion of Shih Tzu breeding behind the Lhasa Apsos of today. Indeed the writer believes that the vast majority of breeders in the UK would be astonished to know that, through the American influence in some more recent British breeding programmes, that same Shih Tzu ancestry is now uncomfortably close on British shores too!

News-Clips

'Smallest of the native breeds of Tibet, that exotic land of Lamas and lost horizons, is the quaint little Lhasa-Apso. Barely a dozen pounds in weight this canine mite is regarded in Tibet as a bringer of good luck – a sort of doggy talisman. Variously known as Sheng Tou, Tibetan Poodle and by nearly a dozen other names.... Although new foreign breeds usually take many years to catch the public eye the Lhasa-Apso has already created enormous interest among fanciers of small dogs.'
The 'Tail-Wagger' Magazine, December 1938

'The true Tibetan dogs are amazingly hardy, and their alertness and vivacity caused them to be called Terriers in India, though their appearance is far from a terrier ... and at the tip of the tail is a peculiar little kink; this is as distinctive as the kink in a bull-dog's tail.'
The Tatler, 15th February 1933

'The most remarkable dogs on view are the eight apsos from Tibet – snakey dogs with long pale brown hair falling from their heads over the tips of their noses.'
10th May 1933 (re Cruft's)

'Another remark of exceptional interest to me is Mrs Hayes' comment on the black tongue in some Lhassa Terriers. I do not think, as she does, that that suggests a drop of Chow blood, as while the Chow is the only black-tongued breed, I have come across some Eastern dogs which had the same peculiarity – not as a breed but as occasional individuals.' – Our Dogs, 'Foreign Dog Fancies' by Will Hally, 10th June 1932

'The chief result of my visit to the show is that I can now distinguish between a Lhasa Apso, a Shih Tzu and a Chihuahua. Of course you know perfectly well what they look like? No? Well, the first looks like any old lady's woolly dog, the next has so much hair that he has it tied out of his eyes with a hair ribbon, and the last, apparently, chooses to live in a birdcage.' – Lady Mary Peckenham at The Dog Show (undated)

'Apsos have made a good show. They have an entry of 19. They are not entirely new but their admirers are "pushing" them this year.'
The Daily Telegraph, 8th February 1937 (re Cruft's)

'I went to see my favourite dog – Pitter-Patter, owned by Major Mayer. He was bought as a mongrel, for 15s, from a monkey cage in Bedford. We loved him as a mongrel. Then he was discovered, by chance, to be an Apso Lhassa, of whom we had never heard.

A mongrel no longer, he became Prince Hajja of Tibet, registered at the Kennel Club "pedigree and breeder unknown".'
By Hannen Swaffer, The Daily Herald, 7th February 1933

2　The Breed Survives

The Second World War Takes its Toll

As for so many breeds the years of the Second World War caused a severe curtailment of breeding programmes and the Lhasa Apso, once again, struggled desperately to survive.

In her report in *Dog World* of 22nd March 1940, Thelma Gray expressed her concern about a number of 'recent importations' including Tibetan dogs. This was as a result of the Kennel Club's recent announcement to 'breed as few litters as possible'. At the time many breeders felt that the announcement was somewhat premature as a great many dogs had been destroyed: some breeders it seemed 'preferred to know the end of their favourites, rather than find them homes with strangers'.[8] Thelma Gray felt that for the lesser-known breeds this was a real crisis.

Interesting discussions took place in the canine press during the early years of the war, proving that dogs could be fed on foodstuffs which did not deprive human beings. Breeders were urged 'to use common sense, and not to be frightened by the non-dog lovers into restricting production'[8] so that their favourite breeds would still be in their rightful place when the war was over.

Mrs Bailey registered only five dogs with the Kennel Club between 1939 and 1944 and Miss Wild also managed to register five; in the latter case these were from two litters, both by the same sire. Sadly Miss Wild's kennel was struck very severely by hardpad and distemper late in the 1940s and her strain was wiped out. The breed did, however, follow through with some Ladkok and Lamleh dogs owned by the Greigs, these being descended from two of the Baileys' imports, Lhasa and Litsi.

Nevertheless, bloodlines having dwindled so dramatically, when the war finally drew to a close the breed was very thin on the ground and had to be built up again. Thankfully, there was still time to import a handful of dogs from Tibet before the Chinese finally banned all movement of dogs from the country. These new imports were, however, largely of unknown pedigree. In 1946 Lt Col. and Mrs H. V.

Irwin of the Madamswood prefix imported a dog and a bitch from Tibet and, mated together, these produced a litter in May 1947. Interestingly, the Irwins repeated this mating in 1948.

Another import in 1947, this time from India, was Lady Doreen Hope's Hopetoun Figaro, bred by Brigadier Lea in 1942. Mrs P. Leigh imported Tika Rant, a bitch, from Tibet in 1948 but again the bitch's pedigree was unknown. 1949 saw five imports from India and Lady Doreen Prior-Palmer (née Hope) imported Hamilton Tura from the Cuttings in the USA.

As the breed moved into the 1950s Kennel Club registrations increased just slightly, with Madamswood and the Furzyhurst breeding of Miss J. Hervey-Cecil featuring more strongly than other lines at the beginning of the decade. As the fifties progressed Mrs Flo Dudman's Ramblersholt and Beryl Harding's (later Mrs Prince) Brackenbury dogs came to the fore.

Audrey Ferris's 'Tibetan Breeds' notes in *Dog World* of 8th February 1952 clearly expressed the state of the breed at the time with an appeal for support at breed shows: 'For those who cannot attend the shows, there is always a "token entry" for the good of the breed. At 12/6 plus 2/6 benching, this is going to cost considerably less than the minimum of £5 that the exhibiting member is going to spend, whether or not he wins.'[9]

No Lhasa Apsos at all were registered with the Kennel Club during the month of January 1952 and the following extract from Audrey Ferris's notes tells its own story:

> 'As most of us know, our great trouble is lack of brood bitches. There are however several good bitches kept as pets. These for their own sake should have one litter, but practical considerations may seem to prevent their owners from mating them. To overcome this Miss Hervey-Cecil has offered to take charge of any bitch Apso, mate her and in due course to have her in her own very excellent kennels for whelping. She would also rear the pups until the normal weaning time and in return she would take one bitch puppy. This is a very practical and generous offer. I hope we shall see use made of it.'

At the Tibetan Breeds Association annual general meeting on 29th January 1952 the Hon. Mrs Irma Bailey, then the Vice-Chairman, complimented the Tibetan Spaniel owners on the great strides they had made in reviving the breed and giving large entries at shows, but put out a plea that owners of Lhasa Apsos should emulate their example.

Her request must have borne fruit for by 1956 Apso owners felt that the breed had gained enough strength to break away from the Tibetan Breeds Association. On 9th May of that year a meeting was held at

Lady Freda Valentine's flat in London to consider this further. This was agreed to and on 18th December the Kennel Club gave permission for the Lhasa Apso Club to be formed. By today's standards, however, the numbers were still very small. At the first AGM, held on 4th January 1957, the Club's membership was twenty-seven, including officers! Although all those involved were interested in Lhasa Apsos, fewer than half of them had show Apsos of their own. Voted into the chair was the Hon. Mrs Irma Bailey.

To begin with, the Club show was held in conjunction with the Ladies' Kennel Association, the only other shows where classes for the breed were on offer being the West of England Ladies' Kennel Society and Cruft's. Nevertheless some lovely trophies which had originally belonged to the Tibetan Breeds Association were passed on to the new club.

In 1959 the name of the breed was changed to Tibetan Apso, for it was the only one of the Tibetan breeds which did not have 'Tibetan' as part of its breed name. This, however, was a change of name which was to last only a decade for by the beginning of 1970 the breed name had reverted to Lhasa Apso.

After the difficulties the breed had encountered since its arrival in the UK prior to the turn of the century, it must have come as a great relief to know that Kennel Club registrations had become sufficient for Championship status once again to be awarded to the breed in 1965. By May 1964 the Kennel Club had confirmed that nine sets of Challenge Certificates would be on offer the following year.

Some Early Dogs of Influence

MARNI (b) Marni was one of a pair of dogs taken from Leh to India by Major Chevinex French, following extensive enquiries as to which was considered to be the approved type. Marni, who arrived in India a good few years prior to the turn of the century, was, in the opinion of Sir Lionel Jacob (of whom we shall read later) 'the best Thibetan Terrier' that he had ever seen. He likens her to Kepwick Tuko (with whom you will also shortly become better acquainted); the particularly interesting point here is that Marni was procured in Leh and Tuko in Calcutta, some considerable geographical distance apart and yet they apparently could have been taken for brother and sister. Marni's show record in India was unbeaten up to the time of her death. The following measurements of Marni may be of interest:

length of head: $6\frac{1}{4}$ ins (15.8 cm)
height at shoulders: 10 ins (25.4 cm)

length of back: 1 ft 7 ins (48.2 cm) (unfortunately we have no way of
telling exactly how the back was measured)
length of ear: $2\frac{1}{4}$ ins (5.7 cm)

BHUTAN (d) Registered with the Kennel Club in 1896, Bhutan was
imported from the Himalayas by the Hon. Mrs McLaren-Morrison.
Although his date of birth and pedigree were unknown Bhutan was
indeed a most charming little fellow and sire of India, his highly
acclaimed son.

Described by his owner as 'the pioneer and only champion in the
breed',[10] Bhutan used to beg at shows, sitting for hours in his decidedly
appealing position. He enjoyed shows, despite the fact that Her Majesty
(whilst still the Princess of Wales) once remarked, 'That little dog is
begging to leave the show.'

Sadly Bhutan contracted distemper whilst begging for the Hospital
Fund and Mrs McLaren-Morrison lovingly describes how he 'fell at
his post, so to speak'. It seems he kept sinking down into a lying
position but would, after a short rest, resume his usual position. 'He
kept his end up to the last,' said his adoring owner, 'and then went
home to die.'[10] Let readers of this book, written nearly a century later,
not forget that charming little character who captured so many hearts
in his own time.

BUSCA BHUTAN (b) Bred by the Hon. Mrs McLaren-Morrison on 2nd
October 1896, her sire was Bhutan and her dam, Busca.

LHASA (d) Lhasa was bred by the Hon. Mrs McLaren-Morrison and
owned by Miss Wild. He was eighteen years old when he died. (Not
to be confused with the Hon. Mrs Bailey's Lhasa in the 1930s.)

KEPWICK TUKO (d) Owned by the familiar Mrs McLaren-Morrison,
Tuko was imported and registered with the Kennel Club in 1901. He
was the dog of that time which 'was accepted by judges as the standard
of the breed in England'.[11] Iron grey in colour he stood 'so low on his
legs that, when in coat, it is impossible to tell whether he is standing
or lying down'.[11] Tuko is the little fellow who originated from the
market cart and of whom we read in Chapter 1. (Note: some sources
refer to this dog as Kepvich Tuko which I believe to be the result of
an original misprint.)

CH. LITTLE DARGEE (d) Bred by the Hon. Mrs McLaren-Morrison in
October 1904, his sire was Terung and his dam, Nariani.

'Lhassa Terrier' – India. These two delightful photographs show India (left) in all his glory and (right) and in 'winter coat'. India was owned by the Hon. Mrs McLaren-Morrison.

INDIA (d) Another dog owned by Mrs McLaren-Morrison and a son of Bhutan. India was black and white with rather dark, very expressive eyes. Interestingly his coat was described as 'long, straight and soft' and his ears as 'drooping and silky'.[11]

In 1907 India was described as 'typical of the breed' and as 'perhaps the best of the breed seen hitherto in England'. India was, however, very markedly different in type from Tuko so it appears that even around the turn of the century there were differences of opinion as to which was the more typical specimen of the breed!

CH. RUPSO (d) Imported from Shigatse in 1907, Rupso was the United Kingdom's very first champion in the breed and was winner of championships four years running, from 1908 to 1911. Rupso's height at shoulder was just a fraction over 10 ins (25 cm). He was owned by Mrs E. G. Webster, and after his death in 1917 his body was preserved in the dog section of the British Museum, now at Tring, where it remains to this day.

DOOMA (b) Of unknown pedigree but registered with the Kennel Club by Mrs W. Corfield in 1912, Dooma's great claim to fame was that she beat Ch. Little Dargee at the Ladies' Kennel Association Championship Show in 1914. (Ch. Dargee was by then ten years old so must have enjoyed an extraordinarily successful show career!)

TASHI (b) Imported by Mrs McLaren-Morrison from India and released from quarantine in England in 1929. In India she had won top honours and was declared to be 'most perfect'. Tashi was 'almost self white' and, had Challenge Certificates been on offer for the breed in England, Mr Hally felt quite sure she would have been a champion.

TOMMO (d) Tommo, owned by Mrs McLaren-Morrison, was described in 1929 as 'the most typical Lhasa in this country, with his short legs, immense paws, heavy coat and massive head'.[12]

LHASA (d) Imported from Tibet by the Hon. Mrs Irma Bailey, his pedigree, breeder and date of birth were unknown. Lhasa was registered with the English Kennel Club in 1931. Until 1934 Lhasa was unbeaten in the 'breed', his record being broken by his son, Satru, at the Ladies' Kennel Association Show at Crystal Palace in May 1934. The judge on this eventful occasion was Col. Bailey!

LITSI (b) Another of Mrs Bailey's Tibetan imports, Litsi was bred by Captain J. A. Nevill. Her sire was Chimtru and her dam, Imotru.

TSITRU (d) Tsitru was imported by Mrs Bailey and was by Satru and Apso, her original pair. Tsitru was born in March 1926 and registered in this country in February 1931.

PEMA (b) A daughter of Itru and Litsi, Pema was also imported from Tibet and bred by Mrs Bailey on 2nd November 1927.

TAKTRU (d) and DROMA (b) The Hon. Mrs Bailey imported these two into England from Tibet in 1928; both were later owned by Mrs Dudley.

SATRU (d) Considered to be a particularly fine specimen, Satru was bred by the Hon. Mrs Bailey in 1932 and was owned by Miss Wild. Golden in colour, Satru had an excellent show record and was undoubtedly one of the leading dogs of his time and indeed one of the most successful exhibits ever benched. His sire was Lhasa and his dam, Litsi, both of whom were imports.

SONA (b) Bred in 1933 by Mrs A. C. Dudley and owned by Miss Wild, Sona was said to be the best bitch to have been seen in England. She was said to have a typical and beautiful head, and correct furnishings. Golden in colour she was prized also for her black ear-tips, black nose and very dark, intelligent eyes. Sona and Satru were famous for their

Taktru and Droma. Imported to England by the Hon. Mrs Bailey and later owned by Mrs A. C. Dudley.

success in brace classes and must have made a very splendid pair.

Sona's death was recorded in the canine press on 4th June 1948 when she had almost reached the age of sixteen years.

TARGUM (d) Another dog owned by Miss Wild, Targum was described as having a magnificent head 'of fine type'. He was of a beautiful red colour and though not shown a great deal due to an illness, he often joined Sona and Satru as a 'team'. Targum's sire was Lhasa and his dam, Drenjong Droma.

ZARA OF LADKOK (d) Owned by Mrs A. R. Greig, his sire was Lhasa and his dam, Pema. Zara met with substantial success in the show ring from the age of eight months and was much in demand as a stud.

MINZONG OF MADAMSWOOD (b) and DZONGPEN OF MADAMSWOOD (d) Bred in Tibet of unknown pedigree, these two dogs were imported to Britain by Lt Col. and Mrs H. N. Irwin. They were registered with the Kennel Club in 1947.

TOMU (b) Tomu gained her fame from Col. Duncan's enchanting little

Sona and Satru with some of their trophies.

Targum. Another of Miss Wild's successful dogs, here shown in his full show-coat.

Zara of Ladkok. An important stud dog in his time, Zara was owned by Mrs A. R. Greig.

book entitled, *Tomu From Tibet*. Tomu originally hailed from Lhasa but had been taken to the Bodnath Temple in Kathmandu, Nepal, where she was given to Col. Duncan by her fond owner, a Chinese Lama. Her sandy-coloured hair was long and matted at this time and, trotting meekly behind Col. Duncan, she left the temple attached to a rope used as a lead. Clearly Col. Duncan was much taken by Tomu's adaptability: she travelled well in the car and made the long journey back to England by train. She showed no signs of nervousness or distrust. Tomu was thought to be about two or three years old when she came from Tibet but her pedigree, breeder and date of birth were not known. She was registered with our Kennel Club in February 1948.

Unfortunately Tomu did not especially enjoy showing: she objected to the vet examining her at the show and disliked the noise. In an 'Any Variety' class she found herself placed between an Irish Wolfhound and a Great Dane. Colonel Duncan tells us that 'This was really too much for her, so that when I had to show her off by walking her across the show ring, she dragged her tail, which normally she carried well curled over her back, along the ground behind her, in the manner of a dowager duchess's train at a dinner party in Victorian times.' Although efforts were made to mate her to a dog imported from Tibet no puppies resulted. Clearly Col. Duncan was saddened by this, for he thought her to be 'an exceptionally good specimen of a true Lhasa Apso'.

ANG LHAMO (b) Was bred in September 1955 by the famous Tenzing Norgay who climbed Everest with Edmund Hillary. Ang Lhamo's sire was Kangra but her dam 'unknown'. She was owned by Mrs J. C. Henderson.

HAMILTON DEWATAS (d) Was imported from the USA by the Hon. Mrs Bailey in 1959. Bred by Mrs Cutting, Dewatas' sire was Am. Ch. Hamilton Kalon and his dam, Am. Ch. Hamilton Den-Sa.

JIGMEY THARKAY OF RUNGIT (d) Sire of the renowned Ch. Brackenbury Gunga Din of Verles, his date of birth and pedigree were unknown but he had been given to Mrs Jill Henderson by Sherpa Tenzing Norgay. Imported from Darjeeling, there was confusion for a short while with regard to his nomenclature but he was finally registered with the Kennel Club as a Lhasa Apso in March 1957. Although he only remained in the UK for a short while, the fresh bloodline introduced by Jigmey Tharkay was a much needed boost, and his matings to Beryl Harding's Brackenbury Lhotse and Brackenbury Min-Nee proved to have a great impact on the breed. Jigmey Tharkay lived also in Peru and in South Africa where, tragically, he died at the age of sixteen, the result of an injury by guard dogs.

BRACKENBURY LHOTSE (b) Miss Harding's foundation bitch, Lhotse, was the result of the mating between Dzongpen of Madamswood and Minzong of Madamswood. Her influence on the breed is clear from the chart on page 30 which shows the successful dogs bred within just a few generations; naturally many more followed those we see there.

Lhotse was campaigned in the days before Championship status was regained but it is highly relevant to mention that she was very successful in the show ring and won Best of Breed at Cruft's.

CH. BRACKENBURY GUNGA DIN OF VERLES (d) The first British champion after status was regained in 1965. He had the honour of winning the breed's very first Challenge Certificate after Championship status was restored; this was at Cruft's Show 1965 under that famous all-rounder, Bill Siggers. Gunga Din was seven years old when he gained his title but had won well on the show circuit in the previous five years.

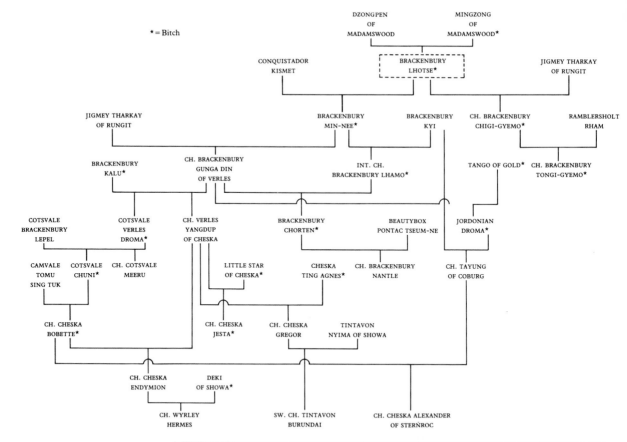

* = Bitch

DZONGPEN OF MADAMSWOOD — MINGZONG OF MADAMSWOOD*

BRACKENBURY LHOTSE*

CONQUISTADOR KISMET — JIGMEY THARKAY OF RUNGIT

JIGMEY THARKAY OF RUNGIT — BRACKENBURY MIN-NEE* — BRACKENBURY KYI — CH. BRACKENBURY CHIGI-GYEMO* — RAMBLERSHOLT RHAM

BRACKENBURY KALU* — CH. BRACKENBURY GUNGA DIN OF VERLES — INT. CH. BRACKENBURY LHAMO* — TANGO OF GOLD* — CH. BRACKENBURY TONGI-GYEMO*

COTSVALE BRACKENBURY LEPEL — COTSVALE VERLES DROMA* — CH. VERLES YANGDUP OF CHESKA — BRACKENBURY CHORTEN* — BEAUTYBOX PONTAC TSEUM-NE — JORDONIAN DROMA*

CAMVALE TOMU SING TUK — COTSVALE CHUNI* — CH. COTSVALE MEERU — LITTLE STAR OF CHESKA* — CHESKA TING AGNES* — CH. BRACKENBURY NANTLE — CH. TAYUNG OF COBURG

CH. CHESKA BOBETTE* — CH. CHESKA JESTA* — CH. CHESKA GREGOR — TINTAVON NYIMA OF SHOWA

CH. CHESKA ENDYMION — DEKI OF SHOWA*

CH. WYRLEY HERMES — SW. CH. TINTAVON BURUNDAI — CH. CHESKA ALEXANDER OF STERNROC

Ch Brackenbury Gunga Din of Verles. Bred by Miss B. Harding and owned by Mr and Mrs Hesketh-Williams, he was the first Champion in the breed after Challenge Certificates once again became available in 1965.

CH.   BRACKENBURY GUNGA DIN OF VERLES

Parents	Grand Parents	G G Parents	G G G Parents
Sire JIGMEY THARKAY OF RUNGIT	Sire *IMPORTED – PEDIGREE UNKNOWN*	Sire	Sire
			Dam
		Dam	Sire
			Dam
	Dam	Sire	Sire
			Dam
		Dam	Sire
			Dam
Dam BRACKENBURY MIN-NEE	Sire CONQUISTADOR KISMET	Sire TSARONG OF FURZYHURST	Sire DZONGPEN OF MADANSWOOD
			Dam ZARA OF FURZYHURST
		Dam TRANA OF FURZYHURST	Sire DANDSH OF LAMLEH
			Dam ZARA OF FURZYHURST
	Dam BRACKENBURY LHOTSE	Sire DZONGPEN OF MADANSWOOD	Sire *IMPORTED FROM TIBET – PEDIGREE UNKNOWN*
			Dam
		Dam MINGZONG OF MADANSWOOD	Sire *IMPORTED FROM TIBET – PEDIGREE UNKNOWN*
			Dam

Bred by Miss Harding (later Mrs Prince) on 18th December 1958 he was transferred to Mr and Mrs F. J. Hesketh-Williams in 1959. Gunga Din's sire was Jigmey Tharkay of Rungit and his dam, Brackenbury Min-Nee.

Some Prominent People in the Breed's History

SIR LIONEL JACOB   was in government service in the Punjab, an expert in Indian dogs he had sufficient interest in the breed to draw up a 'description and standard of points'. Although it must be stressed that this was not an official breed standard, this description was published in the *Kennel Gazette* and *Dog Owners' Annual* in 1901. Lionel Jacob did not agree with the term Bhuteer Terrier but felt that as Lhasa was 'the headquarters of the breed' Llassa Terrier was the most accurate name and preferable to any other. Clearly he was also of the opinion that the breed should be accepted as a distinct one and should be recognised by the Kennel Club.

Perhaps the best way of paying tribute to Sir Lionel Jacob's interest is to reproduce here the guidance he gave in those early years:

'*Head.* Distinctly terrier-like. Skull narrow, falling away behind the eyes in a marked degree, not quite flat, but not domed or apple-shaped. Fore-face of fair length, strong in front of the eyes, the nose large and prominent and pointed, not depressed, a square muzzle is objectionable. The stop size for size about that of a Skye terrier. Mouth quite level, but of the two a slightly overshot mouth is preferable to an undershot one. The teeth are somewhat smaller than would be expected in a terrier of the size. In this respect the breed seems to suffer to an extraordinary degree from cankered teeth. I have never yet seen an imported specimen with a sound mouth.

Ears. Set on low, and carried close to the cheeks, similar to the ears of a drop-eared Skye.

Eyes. Neither very large and full, nor very small and sunk, dark brown in colour.

Legs and Feet. The fore legs should be straight. In all short-legged breeds there is a tendency to crookedness, but the straighter the legs the better. There should be good bone. Owing to the heavy coat the legs look, and should look, heavy in bone; but in reality the bone is not heavy. It should be round and of good strength right down to the toes, the less ankle the better. The hocks should be particularly well let down. Feet should be round and cat-like with good pads.

Body. There is a tendency in England to look for a level top and a short back. All the best specimens have a slight arch at the loin, and the back should not be too short; it should be considerably longer than the height at withers. The dog should be well ribbed up with a strong loin, and well developed thighs.

Stern. Should be carried well over the back after the manner of the tail of the Chow. All Thibetan dogs carry their tails in this way, and a low carriage of stern is a sign of impure blood.

Coat. Should be heavy, of good length and very dense. There should be a strong growth on the skull, falling on both sides. The legs should be well-clothed right down to the toes. On the body the hair should not reach to the ground, as in a show Yorkshire; there should be a certain amount of daylight. In general appearance the hair should convey the idea of being much harder to the eye than it is to the touch. It should look hard, straight, and strong, when to the touch it is soft, but not silky. The hair should be straight, with no tendency to curl.

Colour. Black, dark grizzle, slate, sandy, or admixture of these colours with white.

Size. About 10 ins or 11 ins [25–28 cm] height at shoulder for dogs, and 9 ins or 10 ins [23–25 cm] for bitches.'

We shall discuss the official standard a little later on and when we do it will, I believe, be interesting to reflect upon some of Mr Jacob's initial observations.

THE HON. MRS MCLAREN-MORRISON   played such a terribly important part in the establishment of many foreign breeds in the UK, not only the Lhasa Apso; in England she was the acknowledged authority on Central Asiatic dogs. Having imported Bhutan from the Himalayas in

1896 and bred and owned, along with other Lhasa Apsos, Ch. Little Dargee, she was the earliest known exponent of the breed in this country. Her husband took part in the Younghusband expedition.

MISS MARJORIE WILD had Lhasa Apsos in her family as early as 1901 (or possibly 1900) but she did not begin showing and breeding until 1914. Miss Wild continued exhibiting under her Cotsvale prefix until her death early in 1971. Sadly ill-health prevented her from fulfilling one of her life-long ambitions, to judge at Cruft's. She was to have judged the breed there in 1971.

In her personal notes, written in the 1930s, Miss Wild said, 'Lhasas are almost uncanny in their intelligence, and are very long livers. They are late developers, they rarely acquire their full coat, beard or fringes until three or four years of age. They are also some of the cleanest and most companionable dogs to possess.'

LT COL. E. BAILEY AND THE HON. MRS IRMA BAILEY One could have written little about the history of the breed without reference to the Baileys and so the reader will already have become acquainted with these people to whom we owe so much. Indeed it was the Baileys who brought the word 'Apso' into use in the West. Interestingly, in 1913 Captain Bailey (as he was then) joined Captain Morshead in charting an authoritative map of Tibet. Together they collected several new butterflies and discovered a blue poppy known now to enthusiastic gardeners as *Meconopsis baileyi*.

Irma Bailey gave an Apso dog, Chang-Tru, to Lady Freda Valentine on the occasion of her wedding in 1933, the two ladies having been friends since girlhood.

The Hon. Mrs Bailey died at the age of ninety-two on 19th April 1988 having survived her husband by twenty-one years.

LADY FREDA VALENTINE CBE has been involved with Apsos since the 1930s and has retained her interest in the breed ever since. She was involved in the discussions for the original division of the Tibetan breeds in 1934 and, indeed, it was at her Green Street home that the various breed standards were thrashed out. Again, in 1956, Lady Freda played hostess in her London flat when the meeting took place with a view to establishing the Lhasa Apso Club as a break-away from the Tibetan Breeds Club. Lady Freda was on the Committee of the newly formed Lhasa Apso Club and, following a long Vice-Presidency, she was appointed President of the Club in 1987. Apart from her keen interest in Lhasa Apsos, and indeed the other Tibetan breeds (her sister, Lady Vivien Younger, by the way, had a Tibetan Mastiff), she

Chang-Tru. Lady Freda Valentine's enchanting little Apso 'Chang' clearly displays the 'heart shaped tongue' of which Lady Freda has always been so fond.

is also Vice-President of Guide Dogs for the Blind and was their Honorary Treasurer. Lady Freda's Chang-Tru was among the earliest of the breed to be shown under the name of Apso and Lady Freda has a veritable storehouse of memories about him. 'Chang' (pronounced Chung) absolutely adored the snow but hated getting his tummy wet; the cue for him to roll over for it to be dried was when Lady Freda said '*That* girl in Vienna!' – if only readers of this book could see the twinkle in Lady Freda's eye as she recalls her words, and how heartily she laughs at some of Chang's funny little ways. Apparently he would only do his toilet on grass which created enormous problems when, during the war, they evacuated to her sister's house in Scotland and found no grass at the railway station. Oh, those memorable days!

MRS GREIG and her daughter, DR GREIG were best known for their Tibetan Terriers but the breed must be grateful to them for their help in carrying on the line of Mrs Bailey's imports through several Apsos bred and registered under the Ladkok and Lamleh affixes.

Dr Greig's theories on the origin of the Lhasa Apso are worth recounting, although I have not included them in the earlier section concerning the history of the breed for I have found no evidence to substantiate her claims. She believed that originally Tibetan Terriers were given as tributes to the headmen of villages when the Tibetans travelled in convoy to China; such gifts were to ensure that the party would finally arrive in China in safety. It was Dr Greig's belief that the villagers wanted to keep their luck and so they bred the Tibetan Terrier with the Tibetan Spaniel, the latter being the only small dog they had. This, we are told, was how the Lhasa Apso came into being.

Although Dr Greig did not tell us when she thought the above took place, she was clearly referring back several centuries for she tells us of an event, roughly 450 years ago, when some travellers to Lhasa wanted to obtain a 'genuine Holy dog (the Tibetan Terrier)'. Seemingly the Dalai Lama would not part with one and so he sent his Lamas to search the villages to see if a shaggy dog had been bred which the foreigners would accept. The Lamas found the Lhasa Apso, 'commandeered the lot' and took them to Lhasa. The villagers were so enraged that they, in turn, stormed the monasteries in and around Lhasa and removed all the Tibetan Terriers, replacing them with Lhasa Apsos. Furthermore Dr Greig claimed that many Tibetans in and around Lhasa 'have never seen a genuine Tibetan Terrier and only know the Lhasa Apso as a monastery dog'.

I say again that I have not been able to find evidence to support Dr Greig's theories but, nevertheless, I felt they should be included so that we may keep our horizons open when we consider the history of our breed.

MAJOR SCOTT COCKBURN had a grey and white dog and a golden bitch, Dzong-Pon and Dorje Pamo, presented to him by the Dalai Lama. These he registered with the English Kennel Club in 1934. Both Apsos met with substantial success and provided useful fresh bloodlines for they were not related to each other, neither were they related to any other dog in the UK at the time of their importation.

MRS FLORENCE DUDMAN owner of the Ramblersholt prefix, bred on a small scale and helped to keep the breed alive in the years after the Second World War. She kept mainly dogs and bred to a large extent in conjunction with Miss Hervey-Cecil who kept bitches. Together they managed to retain some lines back to the Ladkok and Lamleh dogs. The following notes, written on the back of the pedigree of Gay Don of Ladkok (bred by Dr and Mrs Greig and owned by Flo Dudman) make interesting reading. Although the notes are undated, Gay Don was born in 1956, so it is likely that that which follows was written in the late 1950s or possibly the early 1960s:

> 'Mrs Greig was the owner of the prefix Ladkok, was one of the founder members of the Tibetan Breeds Association and helped to establish the then Lhasa Apso – later called Tibetan Apsos – as a separate type from Shih Tzus. These latter were not admitted as from Tibet – but from Western China.
>
> Mrs Greig also imported the best Tibetan Spaniel ever, out of Tibet, and others.
>
> Dr A. R. H. Greig, her daughter, was responsible for sending home to England the Tibetan Terrier, and establishing the breed in Europe and USA.
>
> Mrs Daisy Greig (her sister) now has the Ladkok prefix and the Apso interest. Mrs Greig died in 1961 aged ninety-eight.
>
> The Hon. Mrs Eric Bailey and her husband Col. Bailey brought home Lhasa and Litsi and worked to establish the breed in England and founded the Tibetan Breeds Association which then also included Tibetan Mastiffs. Now the three remaining breeds have their own clubs: the Tibetan Spaniel, Tibetan Apso, Tibetan Terrier. Major Meyer, The Lady Freda Valentine and the Baileys remain of the pre-war club.
>
> Unfortunately these latter had no luck breeding after the initial litters, the war intervened. Resurrected after the war, things have now begun to really move.'

Regrettably Mrs Dudman was another who was to have judged the breed at Cruft's but died very shortly beforehand.

MISS J. HERVEY-CECIL of the Furzyhurst prefix bred largely in conjunction with Florence Dudman as outlined above.

TENZING NORGAY a life-long lover of animals, was given two Lhasa Apsos by Lamas in Tibet and Tenzing was made to promise that he would not part with one of them. This one he named Ghangar, after the monastery, the other, Tasang. He took both with him to Darjeeling and although he later gave Tasang to his old friend Angtharkay, Ghangar apparently ran the household along with Tenzing's wife. According to Mukhandi Lal, Tenzing eventually founded a kennel of Lhasa Apsos in Darjeeling, based on a nucleus of Ghangar and Yankee who was to become a champion. Tenzing Norgay took a keen interest in the breed on his visits to the UK.

MRS JILL HENDERSON had been secretary to the Himalayan Climbing Club in Darjeeling and was given two Apsos by Tenzing Norgay. Ang Lhamo, bred by Tenzing, was registered with the English Kennel Club in December 1956 and Jigmey Tharkay of Rungit, who was to become the sire of Ch. Brackenbury Gunga Din, was registered in March of the following year.

MRS BERYL PRINCE (née HARDING) first joined the Tibetan Breeds Association in 1951 and was elected onto the committee the following year. It was in 1952 that she was asked if she would look after Dzongpen and Minzong of Madamswood whilst Col. and Mrs Irwin went abroad. Whilst abroad, and bearing in mind that the dogs were to be looked after at no cost, Miss Harding (as she was then) could mate them and keep all but one dog puppy. This was done. The mating resulted in three puppies, of which she kept Brackenbury Lhotse, grand-dam of Ch. Brackenbury Gunga Din of Verles. The other bitch, Brackenbury Nuptse, went to Mrs Dudman.

Miss Harding, as she was then, received her kennel training at Bellmead where they wanted her to stay on as an instructor. However, she became a veterinary nurse and then opened her first boarding kennel in Uxbridge, where she had such notable clientele as HRH Princess Marina, Duchess of Kent, Princess Katherin of Greece and Lady Doreen Prior-Palmer. Miss Harding later lived in Buxted and in North Wales and spent some months with Miss Wild, for whom she exhibited many Apsos carrying the Cotsvale prefix. Ch. Cotsvale Anna, a bitch of a glorious red colour, was bred by Miss Wild but owned by Mrs Prince; she apparently travelled everywhere with her owner. Other bitches of which she was especially fond were Min-Nee and Lhotse. It has perhaps been little known in the breed that Mrs Prince also exhibited Irish Wolfhounds and certainly made at least two of them champions.

In 1977 she married a life-long friend, LIEUT COL. T. PRINCE, a gentleman dear to many of our hearts, especially for the many years of valued service he gave to the Lhasa Apso Club as its Treasurer. The Colonel had had Kerry Blues and Standard Smooth Dachshunds and following twenty-six years as Treasurer of Southern Counties Canine Association he became its President in 1984. Lieut. Col. Prince's special favourites were Ch. Saraya and Ch. Kangri, who was the last of Mrs Prince's champions and who now carries the Brackenbury flag in the USA. Apart from his canine interests Lieut. Col. Prince led a very full army career which included the Battle of the Somme and, interestingly, he is also President of O'Brien's Scout Group, the only one, he tells me, which has a name. Lieut. Col. Prince still lives in Uxbridge with two Lhasa Apsos but, sadly, Beryl Prince died on 29th June 1985, three days following her seventy-seventh birthday.

In the words of Stanley Chandler, when he wrote of Mrs Prince in the 1980 edition of the Lhasa Apso Club's booklet, 'Wherever long-standing enthusiasts of Lhasa Apsos gather, be it in Westminster (New York), the Sidney Royal (Australia), Cruft's (London), or even Khatmandu (Nepal) Dog Shows, the name of Brackenbury is bound to be mentioned.'

Mrs Beryl Prince (then Miss Harding) judging at Hove Championship Show, August 1967. With her are (left) Mrs F. Sefton and Ch Verles Yangdup of Cheska, Best of Breed and (right) Miss M. Wild and Ch Brackenbury Kan-Ri, Best Bitch.

**Comments Made Following the First Tibetan Apso Show
ever Organised with Tibetan Judges
Held at Tibet House, New Delhi, 11th April 1970**

'They (i.e. Lhasa Apsos) were generally scattered all over Tibet.'

'Although nothing is formally written about Tibetan standards for these dogs, they are so well known to many of us – the lovers of dogs.'

'A close affinity existed between the people of Tibet and their dogs throughout their history. The love of animals is innate in most of them.'

'Apsos should not be fed salty food.'

'The fascination of Tibetans for their animals finds its expression in the pantheon of the ancient Tibetan religion before the advent of Buddhism.'

'Abroad these seem to be known as Lhasa Apsos although we never call them that in Tibet. Probably this is because the first foreigners to acquire Apsos got them from Lhasa.'

'The most prized Apsos are those that have small bodies with long soft coats. . . .'

'The average life span of an Apso is fourteen to sixteen years.'

'To keep the Apso to the minimum size, Tibetans feed a puppy with little quantities of meat, vegetables, tsampa, milk and meat soup.'

'A breed that does not carry its tail over the back in a curl is regarded as a bad dog, whereas one that has a tightly curled tail is believed to be faithful to its master.'

'In Tibet dogs are not given baths regularly but once every two months or so the body of the dog is rubbed with moistened sand in order to make its fur soft and shiny.'

'A well cared-for dog is considered even more fortunate
than many human beings.'

3 The Lhasa Apso in Britain Today

Where exactly does the past end and the present begin? I suppose that the present era really begins with the re-allocation of Challenge Certificates in 1965 and with this event we, naturally, connect Ch. Brackenbury Gunga Din of Verles. A difficulty also arises in distinguishing 'prominent people of the past' from those of the present, for some people have indeed been involved with Apsos for so long that they took a part in the past as well as in the present. Lady Freda Valentine, for example, is still to be seen at the Lhasa Apso Club's Committee meetings and shows, and regularly visits Cruft's to watch the breed judging.

So let us open this chapter with a little information about the proud owner of Gunga Din, Mrs Daphne Hesketh-Williams, who served as Secretary of the Lhasa Apso Club for twenty-one years and who, since 1960, has been a breed note correspondent in the canine press. It was in fact her young Staffordshire Bull Terrier, Varmint, who first fell in love with an Apso. He met one, Brackenbury Min-Nee, at a training class and seemingly fell instantly in love. As a result Mrs Hesketh-Williams bought a Min-Nee daughter from Beryl Harding (later Mrs Prince) in February 1959. Little did she know that this, her first Apso, called Gunga Din, was to have such an effect on the breed throughout the world.

Fond are Mrs Hesketh-Williams' memories of that never-to-be-forgotten Cruft's Show of 1965 when Gunga Din was awarded his first Challenge Certificate. Tom Tru was also entered in the eighteen-strong Junior class, a tremendously large class at that time in the breed's history. Apsos were being exhibited 'upstairs' but, despite this, there were rows and rows of people watching as David Hesketh-Williams took Tom into the class – and won! On another occasion Tom was jokingly described as 'a bundle of old washing' by one eminent judge, who gave him the class none the less.

Mrs Hesketh-Williams campaigned her dogs actively in the 1960s and 1970s and made up a number of champions in the UK, whilst others carrying the Verles prefix hold the title of champion abroad. Mrs Hesketh-Williams' last British champion was Belazieth Ja of

At Welks 1965. This photograph shows Brackenbury Gunga Din of Verles being awarded his third Challenge Certificate with Best of Breed, thus making him a Champion. Gunga Din, pictured on the left, is being handled by his owner, Mrs Hesketh-Williams and the judge is Miss M. Wild. Receiving the bitch CC is Miss Harding's Brackenbury Chigi-Gyemo who was to become a champion later that same year.

Verles, born in 1971; she gained her title in 1975 and was linebred to Ch. Verles Tom Tru, a grandson of Ch. Gunga Din.

Mrs Thelma Morgan also became involved with Apsos around the same time and played a large part in reviving the Bhuteer particolours through descendants of Conquistador Kismet. Mrs Morgan's influence on the breed is not always easy to recognise from merely looking at a pedigree, for many dogs of her breeding have not carried her Ffrith affix. However, when one looks more deeply into the breed her influence on the present-day Apso becomes clearly apparent. An owner of Griffons, Maltese and Shih Tzus to begin with, Mrs Morgan became involved with Apsos as a result of writing a thesis on long coats in canines. She acquired Princess of Everest who was, herself, rather inbred and, mated back to her father, Conquistador Kismet, she produced Tara Blue Princess. Following this Mrs Morgan bought a dog of Mrs Dudman's breeding which she mated to Tara, producing Golden Honey. Despite the fact that Golden Honey was born with a golden hue she matured into a grey and white. All this may sound a little complicated to the uninitiated but it is fascinating to see how Mrs Morgan managed to establish her rather distinctive grey and white line. This is very evident in much of today's winning stock behind which Mrs Morgan's breeding has a strong influence and is, undoubt-

Ch Piplaurie Isa-Silvergilt of Hardacre. Sire: Ch Cheska Alexander of Sternroc. Dam: Piplaurie Isa-Rejoycing. Interestingly this grey and white bitch, bred by Mr K. Warrington and owned by Mrs A. Matthews, goes back to Mrs Morgan's breeding on both sides of her pedigree.

edly, shown in such dogs as those of Mr Ken Warrington's Piplaurie breeding.

Mrs Morgan's first champion, Namista Yarsi, bred by Mr and Mrs Lord, was campaigned to his title in 1965, the very first year in which Challenge Certificates were on offer again. Namista Yarsi's sire was Ch. Pontac Adham Tarhib, bred by Mrs Morgan and owned by Mrs D. Spencer; he was crowned the year after his son, in 1966. Although she always took a very active interest in the breed, frequently to be seen at the ringside and at meetings, Mrs Morgan rarely played the part of 'exhibitor' in the few years before her death late in 1988. Happily her daughter, Glenys Dolphin, is a successful breeder in her own right, and still shows Apsos and awards Challenge Certificates in the breed. Mrs Morgan was deeply involved in Lhasa Apso rescue work and, like Mrs Hesketh-Williams, had been a breed note correspondent for many years; she has committed much to paper and many of her interesting articles in club magazines are well worth seeking out.

In the first ten years of renewed Challenge Certificate status forty-five champions were made up, numbers of entries at shows had increased beyond all expectations and a goodly number of new enthusiasts had joined the breed. Not all of these 'newcomers', as they were then, were new to show dogs and some of them brought with them the experience they had already gained in other breeds. How I would love to list everyone who has been successful in breeding and exhibiting

Lhasa Apsos, but in doing so I feel that I may only serve to confuse the new Apso enthusiast of today. By the time this book goes into print the Lhasa Apso Club will have brought out its long-awaited book of champions which will undoubtedly make interesting reading and will fill in some of the gaps which, of necessity, I have to leave out in a book of this nature.

Mrs Anne Matthews, however, cannot go unmentioned for the mark she has made on the breed has been great. She has bred and campaigned a veritable wealth of champions over the years and the breed will ever be grateful for Mrs Matthews' foundation bitch, Ch. Tungwei of Coburg, who was bred by Mr and Mrs J. Mason and who joined the Hardacre kennel in 1965, becoming a champion in 1968. Tungwei was a very dear favourite and interestingly she proved herself capable of producing champions to widely differing stud dogs, indeed the first champion of Mrs Matthews' own breeding was Ch. Hardacre Ang-Tharkay, who also gained his crown in 1968 and was a daughter of Tungwei and Hamilton Dewatas. By 1972 another of Tungwei's daughters, Ch. Hardacre Hedda, had gained her title, her sire being Ch. Verles Tom Tru. Mrs Matthews proudly describes Tungwei as 'a brood bitch to top all others' and remembers fondly how even from her last litter she produced International Champion Hardacre Last Word.

Although not a champion, Mrs Matthews' Hardacre Pied Piper had great influence on the breed and was sire of Ch. Shelaurie Piperman

Ch Tungwei of Coburg. Sire: Brackenbury Kyi. Dam: Jordonian Droma. A favourite at Hardacre, Tungwei was bred in 1964 by Mrs Y. Mason and was owned by Mrs A. Matthews.

Ch Hardacre Cherry at Deelayne. Sire: Hardacre Kandy Kiss. Dam: Himwari Tuesday's Child. Cherry was bred in 1981 by Mrs A. Matthews and is owned by Mrs M. Lewis.
OPPOSITE PAGE
(TOP LEFT) Ch Verles Tom-Tru. Sire: Ramblersholt Rham Dam: Verles Dhomtuk. Bred by Mr and Mrs Hesketh-Williams.
(TOP RIGHT) Ch Hardacre Hitchcock of Belazieth. The second top winning dog of all breeds in 1971.
(CENTRE LEFT) English, Am. and Can. Ch Belazieth's Malcolm. Sire: Ch Hardacre Hitchcock of Belazieth. Dam: Freth Diane. Bred in 1971 by Mr and Mrs R. Richardson who owned him until his death in 1988. Whilst campaigned in the States he was owned by David Bell.
(CENTRE RIGHT) Ch Belazieth's Salt 'n' Pepper. Pepper won a total of 21 CCs. He was born in 1974 and died in 1988, just a few weeks after his sire.
(BOTTOM LEFT) Ch Belazieth's Charlie Farley of Dobriach. Sire: Ch Belazieth's Salt 'n' Pepper. Dam: Ch Belazieth's Honey Amber. Bred by Mr and Mrs R. Richardson in 1975, Charlie was owned by Mr R. Witham and Miss J. Davidson.
(BOTTOM RIGHT) Ch Tabbi Tu of Jonters. Sire: Ch Belazieth's Charlie Farley of Dobriach. Dam: Jonters Tabu. Bred by Mr and Mrs D. Roe in 1979, owned jointly by the author and Miss C. Johnson.

of Hardacre. This latter had the good fortune to win no fewer than twenty-six Challenge Certificates and was awarded Best in Show, all breeds, at Cardiff Championship Show in the mid 1970s, the second Lhasa Apso to achieve this accolade. Ch. Piplaurie Isa-Silvergilt of Hardacre, bred by Ken Warrington and owned by Anne Matthews, achieved a similar feat later that same year and was the first bitch in the breed to become a Best in Show winner at that level. Another of Mrs Matthews' dogs which played an important part in her breeding programme, and had a far-reaching influence both in this country and in Australia, was Am. & Can. Ch. Hardacre Kinderlands Bhu-Sun.

Mrs Matthews obtains great pleasure in Hardacre stock winning for other owners, and indeed a number of successful breeders obtained their foundation stock from Hardacre – these include Rob and Doreen Richardson of the Belazieth Kennels, and Jean Blyth of Saxonsprings fame. In more recent years Irene Chamberlain's Chobrangs and Madaleine Lewis's Deelayne dogs have made their very certain mark in the show ring.

The Richardsons' first Apso was a bitch, Hardacre Gloria of Belazieth, a daughter of the famous Gunga Din and who went on to produce the much-loved Ch. Belazieth's Salt 'n' Pepper. Secondly came a dog, Ch. Hardacre Hedda's litter brother, that splendid showman, Ch. Hardacre Hitchcock of Belazieth, royally bred by Ch. Verles Tom Tru and out of Ch. Tungwei of Coburg. Hitchcock was bought as an

(LEFT) Ch Lingstoc Midas. Sire: Lingstoc The Jester. Dam: Dewell Hannah. This gold and white dog was bred in 1982 by Mrs S. Linge, his owner.

(RIGHT) Ch Alexander of Sternroc. Sire: Ch Tayung of Coburg. Dam: Ch Cheska Bobette. Holder of many breed records, Alexander was bred in 1969 by Mrs F. Sefton by whom he was also owned in partnership with Mrs P. Cross-Stern.

anniversary present for Doreen and was disguised by Rob as a 'boarder' in their kennels for a few days until the day of the anniversary came around! Hitchcock gained his title in 1971 and was the first of many champions from the Belazieth Kennels. The Verles influence in the Richardsons' breeding programme comes from the third of their Apsos, Verles Jogmaya of Belazieth. In more recent years the Richardsons have also imported some American lines to add to their gene pool; these go back to pure Hamilton breeding. Since Hitchcock became a champion this successful kennel has campaigned a further fourteen Apsos to their English titles and many champions owned by other successful exhibitors and breeders carry the Belazieth prefix both in Great Britain and abroad. The photos on page 45, showing six generations of champions from Ch. Verles Tom Tru through to the author's own Ch. Tabbi Tu of Jonters, are interesting in that the reader can see similarities through so many generations.

A bitch bred by the Richardsons, Belazieth's Golden Pride, was the foundation of Mrs Sylvia Linge's notable Lingstoc kennels. This bitch produced Ch. Lingstoc Te-Ti in her first and only litter. Later Mrs Linge introduced an American-bred dog to her breeding programme and mated him back to her English bitches. Mr and Mrs W. J. Weller's foundation bitch was Megreth Mod-y-Cum, bred by Sonia Harvey and going back to some of the Cheska breeding. This bitch, mated to Ch. Belazieth's Salt 'n' Pepper produced Ch. Dewell Ali and formed the basis of their consistent and successful Dewell kennels.

The breed made history in 1973 when, at the Ladies' Kennel Association's Championship Show for all breeds, Ch. Cheska Alexander of Sternroc, bred by Francis Sefton and co-owned and handled by Pamela

Cross-Stern, went Best in Show, the first win of this kind for the breed. This happened only five months after he had become the first Apso to win a group. To add to his fame at this time he also succeeded in winning the Utility Group at Cruft's in 1974. Alexander's success must have been the start of things to come for Apsos are certainly no longer strangers to top awards. He was born in 1969 and was a great ambassador for the breed; to date his record of having been awarded thirty-six Challenge Certificates has only been broken by Ch. Saxon-springs Fresno. Alexander's dam was the much-loved bitch, Ch. Cheska Bobette, owned by Mrs Irene Plumstead who breeds under the prefix of Showa and who campaigned one of Margot Cook's breeding, Ch. Coomar Yaso of Showa, to her title in 1981.

It is interesting to draw attention to a couple of kennels which were founded in Britain and then went on to be equally successful when their owners moved abroad. We have already come into contact with Mrs Francis Sefton in relation to Ch. Cheska Alexander of Sternroc, just one of the many champions carrying Cheska as an affix or suffix in this country in the late 1960s and early 1970s. Mrs Sefton now lives in Australia but still keeps in touch with our activities here in the UK. Paul Stanton's Tintavon kennel was very successful in England before he moved to Sweden, where his breeding met with equal success. Mr Stanton's first champion, in 1971, bred and co-owned by Mrs Sefton, was Ch. Cheska Gregor who went on to produce Ch. Tintavon Golda-meir who was owned and shown by Jim Bainbridge. Gregor, mated to Goldameir, produced Ch. Botolph's Tashi Lhamo who was to

English and International Nordic Ch Ffrith Smoke Cignal. Sire: Ch Sternroc Jaunty Hoagey. Dam: Dynamic Dinah. Smokey was bred in 1983 by Mrs G. Dolphin. He is owned in partnership by Messrs J. Bainbridge & P. Stanton.

become the breed's youngest champion at the tender age of twelve and a half months. Mr Bainbridge continues to breed very successful stock in this country, one of his recent champions, Ffrith Smoke Cignal, having been sent on to Sweden where he continues his winning ways.

Another breeder who made a great contribution to Lhasa Apsos in this country was Mr John Ford. He bred under the Jonters affix and his original dogs incorporated primarily French Annapurna breeding. In order to bring in some more stock going back to pure Hamilton-bred dogs, Mr Ford imported Ch. Anbara Botan of Jonters from Barbara Wood in the USA. 'Bobby' is now owned by Mrs June Frankl whose Nichann breeding meets with consistent success and much of which goes back to Jonters-bred dogs.

Another who has a good deal of Mr Ford's breeding behind her own stock is Elaine Goodman (Tangla) and the author's Modhish dogs, bred in partnership with Carol Johnson, were founded largely on his breeding. Our own dogs also go back to Belazieth and Hardacre lines through our foundation bitch, Ch. Tabbi Tu of Jonters. Until Mrs Di Trudgill's untimely and tragic death in 1987 her Dengill breeding also carried on the Jonters lines very strongly.

Undoubtedly Jean Blyth's Saxonsprings kennel has had a far-reaching influence on the breed both at home and abroad. Originally a breeder of Basset Hounds, Mrs Blyth had already campaigned several very influential Lhasa Apsos to their titles when, in 1977, she imported from the USA a ten-month-old puppy by the name of Orlanes Intrepid; this she owned in partnership with Joan Kendal, his breeder. Intrepid

(LEFT) Ch Anbara Botan of Jonters. Sire: Am Ch Tabu's King of Hearts. Dam: Mysta's Candi Caper. Bred in 1978 in the USA by Mr and Mrs J. Wheeler, Bobby was imported to the UK by Mr J. Ford that same year. In recent years he has been campaigned and is owned by Mrs J. Frankl.

(RIGHT) Ch Jonters Quentin. Sire: Nangso Golden Guinea of Jonters. Dam: Jonters Amaretti. Bred by Mr J. Ford in 1977 by whom he was initially owned, 'Hutch' was later owned also by Mrs D. Trudgill.

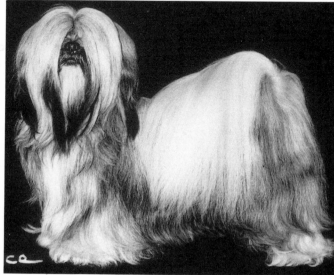

English & American Ch Orlane's Intrepid. Sire: Am Ch Windsong's Gusto of Innsbrook. Dam: Am Ch Orlane's Brandywyne. Bred in 1976 by Mrs J. Kendall, Intrepid is owned by Mrs Kendal and Mrs J. Blyth.

was very soon to become a champion here in the UK where he stayed initially for a period of only two years, during which time he amassed fourteen Challenge Certificates and six Utility Group wins. Intrepid went back to the USA where he was again campaigned with great success, subsequently returning once more to England to remain at the Saxonsprings kennels and to go on to win further high awards in this country.

There can be few Apso enthusiasts throughout the world who have not heard of the two other great winning Saxonsprings dogs, Fresno and Hackensack, both sired by Intrepid. Indeed it was Ch. Saxonsprings Fresno who eventually broke Alexander's record number of Challenge Certificates, and in 1982 she became Pedigree Chum's Dog of the Year, the first time an Apso has ever had this honour. Fresno, presently the holder of no fewer than forty-two Challenge Certificates, is now owned, and still shown, by Geoff Corish who so successfully exhibited her for Mrs Blyth for a large proportion of her career. Ch. Saxonsprings Hackensack is the holder of yet another record for the Saxonsprings kennel by dint of his tremendous achievement of winning Supreme Best in Show at Cruft's in 1984, another 'first' for breed history! Hackensack and Fresno continue to be successfully campaigned well into maturity and continue to meet with substantial success.

Mrs Blyth's influence on the future of the breed has already been seen in dogs shown by many exhibitors who have set up their kennels in more recent years. Mrs Kendal, herself based in the USA, put a

(LEFT) Ch Saxonsprings Fresno. Sire: Eng & Am. Orlane's Intrepid. Dam: Ch Hardacre Not So Dusty at Saxonsprings. Bred in 1978 by Mrs J. Blyth and originally owned by her, in recent years Fresno has belonged to Mr G. Corish.

(RIGHT) English & Irish Ch Saxonsprings Hackensack. Sire: Eng & Am Ch Orlane's Intrepid. Dam: Ch Saxonsprings Chussekuan. Bred in 1979 by Mrs J. Blyth and also owned by her, Hackensack was winner of Supreme Best in Show at Cruft's 1984.

bitch which was to become an English and American champion, Orlane's Luck Be a Lady, in the capable hands of Clive Harrold who had already campaigned some of his own dogs to their English titles.

In 1975 Mrs Sue Ellis set up her Nedlik kennels, since when she has bred seven English champions, others of her breeding holding their titles abroad. All Mrs Ellis's breeding goes back to one of Mrs Blyth's English-bred dogs, Ch. Saxonsprings Zako, and to Scarlet Eris, bred by Mrs Morgan.

So many other breeders are deserving of mention and I can only apologise to those who have indeed had an influence on the breed but to whom I have been unable to pay tribute in these pages. Before closing this section one must, however, mention Mr and Mrs S. Chandler, who brought back their black foundation bitch from India and bred under their Burdyck affix; the stalwart Hetti Wysocki, who has been campaigning her Sursumcorda dogs with consistent success since the late 1960s; and Mrs Rosemary Wallis, who has developed a very distinctive and successful grey and white line which she has often shown in conjunction with Mrs Pauline Torrance. Mrs Maureen Millett's Escafeld breeding and Mrs Tina Lewis's Ragoosa dogs have both had a very certain influence on the breed in the UK and, more recently in Scandinavia. Neither, indeed, is there any doubt that the breeding of Mrs A. Shelley (Nangso), Mr and Mrs R. Holder (Andmac), Mr and Mrs J. Scarll (Timazinti), Mrs P. Brewer-Luiz (Parlu) and Mr R.

Ch Nedlik Pick-A-Pepper of Belazieth. Sire: Ch Belazieth's Salt 'n' Pepper. Dam: Nedlik Cassie. Bred in 1986 by Mrs S. Ellis, he is owned by Mr and Mrs R. Richardson.

Ch Escafeld Danielle. Sire: Sweet Golden Shadow of Lisimo. Dam: Escafeld Chloe. Bred in 1983 by Mrs M. Millett, by whom Danielle is also owned.

English & Danish Ch Ragoosa Mitoyah. Sire: Eng & Irish Ch Saxonsprings Hackensack. Dam: Saxonsprings Amarillo. Bred and owned by Mrs T. Lewis, following a very successful English show career Toyah was exported to Denmark in 1986 where, under the ownership of Mrs T. Staunskaer, she gained her title in three consecutive shows. In 1986 she was also awarded Reserve Best in Show at The Winners Show, Amsterdam.

Witham and Miss J. Davidson (Dobriach) has also made its mark and will continue to do so in generations hence.

Breed Clubs

We have already become acquainted with the way in which the Lhasa Apso enthusiasts broke away from the Tibetan Breeds Association in 1956 and set up their own 'Tibetan Apso Club' under the Chairmanship of the Hon. Mrs Irma Bailey. Mrs Daphne Hesketh-Williams soon became both Secretary and Treasurer and the club grew so fast that the position of Treasurer was eventually passed to the very capable hands of Lieut Col. Prince, who held office until 1985 when Mr Peter Millett took over from him.

The first Club show was held in April 1969 at Oxford, and the judge, Mr Clement-Cuny from France, had an entry which was a world record for the breed: ninety-one Apsos, made up of forty-four dogs and forty-seven bitches. Clearly that day was a great one for the club; everyone felt a tremendous sense of achievement and the lovely trophies, some of which were made of irreplaceable Tibetan silver, were set out on the Tibetan flag. Best in Show went to Mrs Sefton's Tayung of Coburg with Reserve Best in Show and Best Opposite Sex being awarded to her home-bred Ch. Cheska Jesta. Lady Doreen Prior-Palmer, a Vice-President, went along to the show as a spectator, and Miss Wild, also a Vice-President, presented the trophies and rosettes.

1970 brought a change of name to the 'Lhasa Apso Club' and saw the Club's first Championship show, which took place at Sedgley, near Wolverhampton. The judge, all-rounder Mrs Judy de Casembroot, judged seventy-one exhibits and awarded the Dog Challenge Certificate to Ch. Cheska Endymion and the Bitch Challenge Certificate to Ch. Cheska Bobette. The Best of Breed trophy was a Tibetan butter lamp, presented to the Club by its then Patron, the Queen of Sikkim.

The Club went from strength to strength and not until 1981 did the loyal Mrs Hesketh-Williams finally stand down as Secretary, her position being filled by Mrs Margot Cook and later by the author. Recent Chairmen of the Committee of the Lhasa Apso Club have included Mr W. M. Brownlie, Mr S. Chandler, Mrs A. Matthews, Mr R. Witham and Mr S. Chamberlain.

The 1st June 1980 saw the first member enrolled in what was to become the Midland Lhasa Apso Association, thanks to the initial impetus of Mrs G. Dolphin, Mrs M. Holder and a group of enthusiasts in the Midlands area. The Association benefited greatly from the support of Mrs T. Morgan and many others who worked hard to establish it in its formative years. From the outset Mrs G. Dolphin was Secretary, later handing over to Mr T. Richardson. After a number

Lady Freda Valentine cuts the cake in celebration of the Lhasa Apso Club's 30th Anniversary. The event took place at the Club's 18th Championship Show and with Lady Freda are the Club's Vice-Presidents, Officers and Committee Members.

of Limited and Open shows the Association was granted permission to hold its first championship show in 1985 when Mrs T. Morgan awarded Best in Show to Mrs Wallis's Follow That Dream of Viento and Reserve Best in Show to Mrs S. Ellis's Ch. Nedlik An An.

1987 saw the formation of yet another club, the South Eastern Lhasa Apso Society, headed by Mr R. Witham as Secretary. This new and enthusiastic society's first Open show took place at the beginning of 1989 and was judged by Mrs Anne Matthews.

Rescue

Sadly it would not be possible to close this chapter without mention of the rescue work which is carried out by the various clubs. Suffice it to say that for those who have real and genuine difficulty in keeping their Apsos the club secretaries are able to put people in touch with those who will certainly try to help. I must, however, stress that rescue sections of the clubs are not merely convenient outlets for disposing of Apsos who have perhaps outgrown their usefulness. The rescue services are called upon far more frequently than one would wish but are particularly useful in cases of bereavement or, for example, the owner's sudden disability. Often if a difficulty arises it can be helpful to have someone with whom to talk through the problem and from whom one can seek guidance but, naturally, if you do find yourself in a difficult situation the first person to contact is the breeder of the dog in question. If you have bought from a reputable breeder you should find that he or she will be pleased to listen and, in many cases, situations can be resolved before they become too traumatic.

4 The Kennel Club Breed Standard

The UK Kennel Club's Breed Standard has been revised a number of times over the years but here we shall concern ourselves with the most recent rewrite, which was printed in 1986.

It is relevant to mention that well before the Kennel Club reprinted the Standard, the breed clubs were consulted and a joint meeting was held for the committee members of the two clubs which existed at that time.

Changes made to any Standard will always be met with a difference of opinions and it would be a rare thing if everyone could agree with every change made. But let us consider, too, that everyone's interpretation of a standard will differ just slightly, for a standard can only create a word-picture of the breed, outlining those points which make the breed a Lhasa Apso as opposed to a Tibetan Terrier or, indeed, an Irish Wolfhound.

Before considering each particular point of the Standard let us look at it as a whole. However well we feel we know our Standard it always does us good to re-read it for it is surprising what little points we forget or perhaps conveniently overlook:

General appearance Well balanced, sturdy, heavily coated.

Characteristics Gay and assertive.

Temperament Alert, steady but somewhat aloof with strangers.

Head and skull Heavy head furnishings with good fall over eyes, good whiskers and beard. Skull moderately narrow, falling away behind the eyes, not quite flat, but not domed or apple-headed. Straight foreface with medium stop. Nose black. Muzzle about 4 cm (1½ ins), but not square; length from tip of nose roughly one third total length from nose to back of skull.

Eyes Dark. Medium size, frontally placed, oval, neither large nor full, nor small and sunk. No white showing at base or top.

Ears Pendant, heavily feathered.

Mouth Upper incisors close just inside lower, i.e. reverse scissor bite. Incisors in as broad and as straight a line as possible. Full dentition desirable.

Neck Strong and well arched.

Forequarters Shoulders well laid back. Forelegs straight, heavily furnished with hair.

Body Length from point of shoulders to point of buttocks greater than height at withers. Well ribbed. Level topline. Strong loin. Balanced and compact.

Hindquarters Well developed with good muscle. Good angulation. Heavily furnished with hair. Hocks when viewed from behind parallel and not too close together.

Feet Round, cat-like with firm pads. Well feathered.

Gait/Movement Free and jaunty.

Tail High set, carried well over back but not like a pot-hook. Often a kink at end. Well feathered.

Coat Top coat long, heavy, straight, hard neither woolly nor silky. Moderate undercoat.

Colour Golden, sandy, honey, dark grizzle, slate, smoke, parti-colour, black, white or brown. All equally acceptable.

Size Ideal height: 25.4 cm (10 ins) at shoulder for dogs; bitches slightly smaller.

Faults Any departure from the foregoing points should be considered a fault and the seriousness with which the fault should be regarded should be in exact proportion to its degree.

Note Male animals should have two apparently normal testicles fully descended into the scrotum.

Reproduced by permission of the Kennel Club.

In an ideal Lhasa Apso mouth the lower canines should fit neatly just inside the upper ones and the incisors (6 at the top and 6 at the bottom) should be in as straight a line as possible.

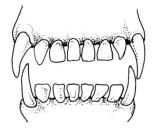

The following diagrams show how the incisors should and should not be placed – the dog is facing to the left in every case: –

a tight reverse scissor bite is correct for the Lhasa Apso

overshot – incorrect

undershot – here the lower jaw protrudes too far out

level – the breed standard no longer requires this bite for the Lhasa Apso

this *scissor bite* is more usual in most breeds with longer forefaces but is incorrect for the Lhasa Apso

The initial overall description of the Apso, given in **'General Appearance'** briefly conjures up a picture of a dog which is neither extreme nor exaggerated in any way and which does not have a delicate bone structure as do some of the Toy breeds. Indeed, we must always bear in mind that here in the UK the Lhasa Apso is included in the Utility Group, not in the Toy Group as it is in some countries abroad. 'Heavily coated' needs no further clarification at this stage.

As we move on to **'Characteristics'** and **'Temperament'** we learn, in just a few words, quite a lot about the mentality of this little dog and I think the description of the word 'gay' in the *Longman's Dictionary* is very apt – 'cheerful, happy, full of fun'. But if this little fellow is 'assertive' it indicates a certain strength of character; indeed the Apso is very often quite capable of showing just who is boss. 'Alert' means that he is quick to see and to act, that he is watchful and ready to deal with danger, vigilant.

The Standard then goes on to tell us that he is 'aloof with strangers' but this is qualified by the word 'steady', meaning that although he is perhaps somewhat reserved or 'stand-offish' with those he does not know, his temperament is well controlled. Nothing in the Standard indicates that he should be aggressive with strangers, but neither should he leap all over them with amorous kisses at their approach. The very friendly character may be more appealing in the show ring but it is not correct; I rather think the puppy which has to be trained to tolerate the judge going over him is the one which expresses the true Apso temperament.

Although I have said that here we are to concern ourselves with the current Breed Standard, I feel it relevant to mention that in the most recent re-write the word 'aloof' was chosen to replace the word 'chary', but, having been party to the meetings which took place within and between the breed clubs prior, I can vouch for the fact that the change was made only after a great deal of discussion. Chary means 'cautious or shy of' and it was felt that in a dog now destined for the show ring this aspect of its character should not be taken too literally.

The Breed Standard pays a great deal of attention to **'Head and Skull'** and, this being the case, we, too, must consider this aspect of the Apso very carefully. There is reference to 'heavy head furnishings' but not to a heavy head beneath! Indeed it is stated quite clearly that the skull should be 'moderately narrow, falling away behind the eyes'. The latter is a phrase which is not entirely clear at first glance but it means that the bone behind the eye (i.e. from the outer corner) should not protrude as it would in breeds with a more domed skull and a rounder eye. The top of the skull should be a happy medium between the flat skull of the Chow or the Pekingese and the domed and apple-headed skulls of breeds such as the King Charles Spaniel and the Chihuahua.

The foreface is to be 'straight', meaning that it should not be upturned but nor should it be downfaced. Ideally the uppermost tip of the nose should be in line with the lower eye rim. If the foreface is at the correct angle the stop will usually also meet the requirements of the Standard. In aiming to achieve a 'medium stop' we do not require a protuberance at the front of the skull, such as is to be found on some of the breeds with domed or apple-shaped skulls.

About the length of the muzzle, and the fact that it should not be 'square', the Standard is quite specific. We are even given the proportion we should aim for in relation to the total length of the skull. Although the occiput is not actually mentioned, this is what is meant by 'back of skull', i.e. the bony 'knobble' just at the back of the skull. If one does not know exactly where to measure to there can always be a tendency to misinterpret the wording to suit the dog! To keep the 'mediumness' of foreface which we have in our breed is not an easy thing to do, for nature will always strive to revert to the norm; so it is that scissor bites will keep creeping in. Although we are not yet on the subject of mouths it is largely the length of foreface which determines this feature. It is, in fact, almost impossible to analyse the various features of the body in isolation; this we shall see even more clearly as we progress through the Standard. Having said that, we shall come to nose pigment and head furnishings in conjunction with other features later on.

The **'Eyes'** are described as 'dark' and there is no clarification to say that lighter eyes are permissible in some colours; they are definitely not. Certainly light eyes seem to be becoming increasingly common in the breed, especially in the lighter coloured dogs (though not, thankfully, in all of them). The depth of colour in the Apso's eye adds to that lovely Oriental expression of the breed, something simply not found in a dog with a light eye. The Standard is, admittedly, not always clear but it is so with reference to the eyes and there is, therefore, no excuse to deviate. Due to the luxurious wealth of hair which cascades over the face it is all too easy to disguise an untypical eye and one can find so many disappointments when one peeps behind the furnishings.

If the head shape is correct the eyes, too, will meet the requirements of the Standard. We are seeking a 'medium' sized, 'oval' eye which is 'frontally placed'; this size, shape and placement of eye fits naturally into the skull of the breed. The fact that no white is called for 'at base or top' emphasises the required 'oval' shape, for it is in a round eye that white shows surrounding the pupil. A round eye fits into a more rounded skull shape than we require in the Apso.

Little is said in the Standard concerning the **'Ears'**; the wording is concise, to say the least, but 'pendant', believe it or not, tells us quite a lot. It means that the ear should be at least moderately low set, for if the ears are set too high the ear flap would, of necessity, tend to have some lift to it and so the ears would stand slightly off from the skull. In this section what the Standard does not say is just as important as what it says.

And now we move to that very controversial subject, the **'Mouth'**. Why it is controversial I am never quite sure, for the Standard is specific enough: 'upper incisors close just inside lower, i.e. reverse scissor bite'. What is required in an ideal bite is that the back of the teeth in the lower jaw just touch the front of the teeth in the upper jaw; there should not be a gap between top and bottom teeth or the mouth will be too undershot. Granted, it is difficult to achieve and to maintain a perfect bite for this breed, but the bite described in the Standard is that for which we should aim.

Two further clarifications are given in the Standard, that the incisors should be 'in a broad and as straight a line as possible' and that full dentition is 'desirable'. These two go hand in hand, for it is primarily in the narrower jaws that one gets missing teeth – there not being sufficient space for them all to fit in, nature may have chosen to leave one or two out. Sometimes, if the jaw is not sufficiently broad, one does find six incisors between the canines but the teeth are very jumbled. Apart from the fact that a narrow jaw does not, usually, give the desired expression for the breed, teeth in a 'jumbled mouth' are usually more prone to early decay. Full dentition in the Lhasa Apso is as for the canine species in general:

	incisors	canines	pre-molars	molars
upper jaw	6	2	8	4
lower jaw	6	2	8	6
total = 42				

The diagrams on page 57 show how, in the ideal mouth, all six incisors in each jaw fit neatly between the canines of the corresponding jaw.

The **'Neck'** is to be 'strong and well arched'. Necks in general seem to be increasing in length and, as neck and carriage of head is linked with shoulder placement, this is not undesirable. However, the Standard does not call for a long neck and we are therefore not aiming for over-long or swan necks, which would be uncharacteristic. Shoulder placement is important for not only does it have a bearing on head carriage but also on movement. The Standard tells us that the shoulders should be 'well laid back', indicating a reasonable slope backwards to the withers. The shoulder blades will also angle in so that there is only a fairly narrow gap between the uppermost points of the scapuli at the withers. An Apso with upright shoulders cannot achieve the free movement which is desired for the breed, as his forehand stride will be limited and will (unless he is also straight in stifle!) not complement his hind movement.

In the section concerning **'Forequarters'** we are also told that the forelegs are to be straight. It is very difficult to breed for legs which are absolutely straight if we are to keep height, rib shape and shoulder placement typical of the breed. Nevertheless that is what we must aim for and individual breeders must assess the strengths and weaknesses of their stock to determine how best they can achieve and retain straight fronts within their breeding programmes. A noticeable bow must be avoided as should the tendency to be 'out at elbow', for both such forms of construction will play havoc with movement. An 'East–West' front, with the feet pointing outwards, is definitely not called for, though I am tempted to say that it is becoming prevalent in the breed. Such a forehand construction should be avoided for it is not easy to breed out once established; let us aim to have all four feet pointing in the direction in which they are going!

We move on now to **'Body'**, where we are told that the 'length from point of shoulders to point of buttocks' is to be 'greater than the height at withers'. Unfortunately the Standard fails to tell us by what

proportions:

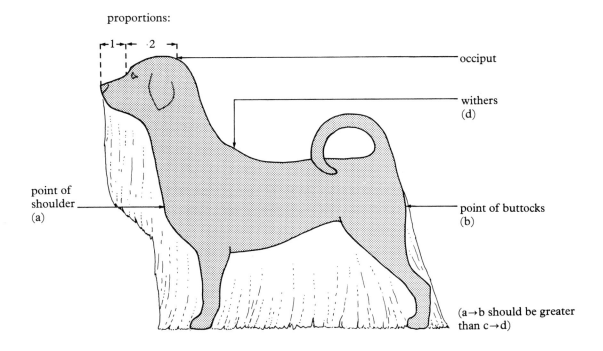

occiput

withers
(d)

point of
shoulder
(a)

point of buttocks
(b)

(a→b should be greater
than c→d)

proportion or measurement the length should be greater than the height; clearly, though, we are not looking for a square dog. The diagram will show you the points from which the measurements are to be taken when assessing this.

The ribs are of great importance in a breed which, in its natural environment, lived at high altitude for the Apso needs plenty of heart and lung room. The Standard requires the Apso to be 'well ribbed' (the word 'up' having been deleted from the most recent Standard). By implication we are therefore seeking a rib-cage which extends well back along the body but also one which is well sprung, not a barrelled rib-cage but not slab-sided either; we come back to that word which I suspect does not exist in any dictionary: 'mediumness'. The rib-cage also needs to be of reasonable depth, reaching virtually to the elbow joint.

The Standard also requires a 'level topline', that is to say that it should neither dip nor roach whilst the dog is standing or when on the move. A poor topline can be the result of hindquarters which are slightly high in comparison with the forequarters, in which case the line slopes upwards towards the back; it is unusual in the extreme to find the reverse. The reason for this excessive height at the back end may be that the bones of the hind legs are too long in proportion to those in the front, or it can be, and often is, because the angulation of the hindquarters is incorrect, usually being too straight in stifle. Again we see how the various parts of the Standard interact with one another and how it is virtually impossible to analyse one section in isolation. A 'strong loin', another feature called for by the Standard, plays its part in helping to keep the topline steady when on the move. If the loin is weak it is only too easy to see the spinal column move up and down like a wave when the dog is in motion. Lastly the section concerning body says 'balanced and compact', which in itself indicates that we are not looking for excessive length from point of shoulder to point of buttocks but that the Lhasa Apso is to be just that, balanced and compact.

Now, when we look at **'Hindquarters'** we are already aware that they should be in proportion to the forequarters for if they are not, even if a clever handler can conceal this whilst standing, it will certainly show up on the move. The Standard asks for 'good angulation', but do take note that the word used is 'good' and not 'excess'. Excessive angulation will again cause the dog to move incorrectly, for the hind legs will be capable of covering more ground than the forelegs and the dog will have to find some way of compensating, most probably by throwing up the feet behind, showing the full pad. It is true that the Apso should show a little of its pad as it moves away but not the entire pad; such movement is not correct for this breed. The Standard requires 'good muscle', again indicating that the breed should be given a fair amount of exercise for an Apso whose exercise is severely limited in order to 'grow coat' will not develop the required muscle.

Lastly in this section of the Standard, the hocks are required to be 'parallel and not too close together' when viewed from the rear. Cow hocks and sickle hocks are therefore not in keeping with the Standard. The hocks being too close together, something else to be avoided, is often coupled with a generally narrow hind construction which can, of course, bring with it whelping problems in the bitch.

The Lhasa Apso's **'feet'** are to be round and 'cat-like' which means that they are similar in overall shape to those of a cat but, in fact, the pads are much closer together in the Lhasa Apso giving rather less flexibility of movement of each digit. None the less the Apso's foot is very capable of gripping, a necessity, no doubt, in his homeland. The feet are to be 'well feathered'.

So very little of the Standard is allocated to **'Gait/Movement'**; it merely states 'free and jaunty' and in the author's opinion the latter of those two words can be taken to mean many different things – and, indeed, sometimes it is! Let us look then at the first word which in itself is rather more clearly explicit. Free implies a certain fluidity of stride, unrestricted and not 'stilted' as, for example, in some of the terrier breeds. I mentioned earlier that in order to develop a straight front there is a tendency also to produce a rather upright shoulder and this will give that same incorrect action of the forelegs when on the move. The very fact that the Apso is longer than it is high gives it a facility for freedom of movement which is not so easy to achieve in the shorter-backed breeds. The dog should move true; there will be a natural tendency to single track but the elbows should not be loose – indeed when the dog is stacked you should be able to feel that the elbows are nice and tightly placed against the side of the rib-cage. In the Lhasa Apso, being 'out at elbow' is a much more common fault than being 'tied', neither of which gives rise to correct movement for in the first instance the dog will plait and weave and in the second it will tend to throw its front legs out. We have already talked about the fact that if the rear quarters are not constructed in a complementary way to the forequarters the dog will always find a way to compensate and, without going into the many different faulty patterns of movement, suffice it to say that the movement will not be free.

Jaunty is a strange adjective to use in relation to movement and I suspect that the word is often used as an excuse for movement in which the Apso bobs up and down or rolls from side to side whilst on the move, both of which are quite incorrect and are caused by less than perfect construction. I resort, as I so often do, to the *Longman's Dictionary,* which, for those who do not know, gives crystal-clear explanations so that words will be easily understood, especially by foreign people. It says: '**jaunty** – (showing that one feels) cheerful, confident, and pleased with life'; for me, that sums it up perfectly.

The **'Tail'** is to be 'high set' and if an Apso's tail is set high enough the dog will feel comfortable with its tail up at all times. It is interesting to observe a litter of young puppies, some of which have better tail sets than others; those with a really good tail set will feel perfectly comfortable with the tail carried well over the back all the while, whilst those with a slightly lower set of tail (albeit not so low as to be noticed as a faultily low set) tend to drop the tail whilst eating. It should be carried well over the back and, again, if the tail is high set it will automatically go well over the back. 'Not like a pot-hook' means that it should not loop up and over in the manner of the handle of a shepherd's crook (pots and tea-pot handles come in such a variety of shapes these days that I am reluctant to use them as an example!). There is 'often a kink' at the end, says the Standard. Sadly that kink is rapidly becoming a thing of the past. On those Apsos in which it is to be found it is just a tiny bend about half an inch (12 mm) or so from the end of the tail – one almost feels one wants to pull it out which, of course, one cannot and must not do, for it is quite firmly bent. It certainly was very characteristic of the breed and I feel a little sad that it is disappearing so fast.

When we go on to discuss coat, let us now also include all those many references to the furnishings which appear throughout the Standard. The **'Coat'** of the Apso is double. The top coat is required to be 'long', 'heavy', 'straight' and 'hard'. It should not be woolly or silky. The words used in this section of the Standard are very descriptive and it is worth bringing the reader's attention to the fact that the word 'hard' is used, not harsh. If the coat were harsh it would have a tendency to break, but a hard coat implies much stronger strands of hair and indeed this often carries a fair amount of natural oil which adds to the weight of the top coat. Indeed the coat of the Lhasa Apso is very unlike most other canine coats and indeed was spun to make clothing in the Apso's mother-land. Let us also keep in mind that the Lhasa Apso's coat acts as a protection not only against the cold but also against heat. For this reason the breed must have an undercoat, although now the wording of the Standard says 'moderate undercoat', not 'dense' as it did until the most recent change. Certain it is that a large proportion of the somewhat softer undercoat is groomed out for the purposes of presentation in the show ring, but we must never breed out the under-coat or we shall, in doing so, dramatically change the very nature of our little friend from Tibet who had to suffer extremes of temperature and needed to be well equipped to do so.

In the Standard there are numerous references to the furnishings: 'good fall over the eyes, good whiskers and beard'; ears 'heavily feathered'; forequarters 'heavily furnished with hair'; hindquarters 'heavily furnished with hair'; feet 'well feathered'; tail 'well feathered'. When we look at these phrases in isolation we see that they do indeed relate to the areas of the Lhasa Apso on which the coat seems to grow in natural profusion, although it is, of course, always a little more difficult to keep good coat on the hindquarters for a variety of reasons. Some dogs also seem to have an infuriating habit of wiping their ears along the floor and walls, thereby rubbing off any lovely long feathering they might otherwise grow!

Strictly speaking, it would be incorrect to say that there is now no preference for **'Colour'** for the Standard lists colours and then states that all are 'equally acceptable'. Thus it is only the aforementioned colours which are equally acceptable and whilst those listed cover a very wide range it is important to note that liver is not included; indeed it would not be possible to include liver if the Standard also requires a black nose for the two just cannot be produced in one animal. In my opinion one of the very appealing features of the Apso is that it comes in such a variety of hues, and it is lovely to see such coat colours in a well-filled class at a show. It is, however, true that differences in overall construction are to a certain extent linked with a difference in colour due, primarily, to the original stock from which they were descended. However, as well-planned breeding programmes continue we shall hopefully see both type and colour merge more closely.

It is highly relevant to mention that the Lhasa Apso Standard does not make allowances for poor pigmentation in lighter-coloured dogs and it is important to keep this in mind when breeding together some of the paler-coloured dogs which, in some cases (not, of course, in all), have a tendency to weak pigmentation or at least a severe 'winter nose'. It is the author's opinion that if the breed is to retain good pigmentation where it already exists, and improve upon it in the future, it is essential just occasionally in breeding programmes to use black dogs or those carrying genes for black.

Whatever the differences of opinion between breeders in the past, it now holds true that all listed colours are held in equal esteem. The important result of this equality of colour is that judges can make their assessment of the dogs before them on the merit of the dog, without paying attention to colour.

'Size' is not quite as straightforward as it appears at first glance. The Standard is clear enough: 'Ideal height: 25.4 cm (10 ins) at shoulder for dogs; bitches slightly smaller.' The key word is 'ideal', which allows for a certain latitude, and indeed we must bear in mind that the American standard allows for a little more height ('10 or 11 inches' (25.4–27.9 cm)). If we have American breeding in this country, which we do, then we have to accept that at this stage in the merge between American and English stock some dogs will slightly exceed 10 ins (25.4 cm). They should definitely not, however, approach the height of the Tibetan Terrier – the difference in height between the two breeds was sorted out long ago! If latitude is allowed upwards, then it is my belief that it should also be allowed downwards, for it is not so many years ago that the English Standard read 'ideal height 9 inches or 10 inches at the shoulder for dogs; bitches slightly smaller'; this was the wording of the 1964 Standard which was effective until 1973. Just think for a moment before forming your own opinion – for example, a $9\frac{1}{2}$ in. (24.1 cm) dog (absolutely correct for the standard of the day) born in 1972 could well have sired litters of puppies up to 1982 and possibly later. This would mean that his sons and grandsons are in the ring today – it takes much longer than one or two generations to change the overall size of dogs within a well-planned breeding programme. Having said all that (!), 10 inches (or 25.4 cm) is the height for which we should aim.

Lastly we come to **'Faults'** and to the **'Note'**. Both sections are common to all Kennel Club Breed Standards – hopefully it is sufficient to say that neither should be overlooked!

5 Why Choose an Apso?

A dog can be many things to many people, but an Apso is a very special kind of dog and, although he may be the perfect companion for many, a Lhasa Apso is not necessarily the right breed for everyone. Let us now try to take an overall look at this endearing little animal to see both his good points and his not-so-good ones. Only in this way can we ascertain whether we should or should not have an Apso (or perhaps several of them) sharing our lives.

Personality

I deal with this aspect first because it is probably the most important consideration, particularly in view of the fact that the Apso is a compact little dog and from a size point of view could therefore fit into virtually any household.

If I say that he is a 'tough' little character, I hope you will not misunderstand me. It has been said time and time again that he is a big dog in a little body, and this description is very apt. He is not a Toy breed in any way. Though small in stature his mentality is that of a much larger dog and he will usually stand his ground against animals of much greater size and weight.

My very first Apso (a male) lived for many years with my two male Afghan Hounds and, despite his diminutive size, he was very much the dominant dog. The only reason I eventually parted him from his two large companions was that I felt the Afghans needed a little peace and quiet in their closing years. There were occasionally fracas, as there are in any happy household, but the little fellow would simply roll himself up in a tiny ball, closely resembling a hedgehog, whilst the bigger boys gave way to their anger. Thankfully our friend the Apso always came out unscathed.

So he is a tough little dog who mixes well but, of course, one must always take the utmost care when introducing one dog to another. Some people keep their stud dogs together, but from personal experience I have always found that males which have been used at stud definitely do not mix with other stud dogs. They may tolerate other males, especially if younger than themselves, and will almost certainly love having a lady about the house. But, just as humans, each one is different and you would be well advised to be prepared for any reaction to a change in circumstances or environment.

Whilst I am certain that Apsos like to have at least one other dog around them, they are indeed very adaptable and if one is to be kept singly as a pet he will usually become very attached to the person or family with whom he lives. He is not, however, a dog who will enjoy spending many long hours alone and perhaps the working family who wishes to have a companion strictly for evenings only would be better advised to consider perhaps a cat or a hamster, rather than any member of the canine species.

An Apso kept as a companion will usually be loving to his owners, but we must always bear in mind that he is not really a lap dog. Though he may seek your comfort and companionship he may, at times, prefer to be alone, usually somewhere almost out of your sight, but where he can still open a beady eye to check that you're still around if he decides he needs you. Most like to take advantage of the furniture, if it's not out-of-bounds, but it is relatively easy to train them to stay at floor level provided that this is done firmly and, ideally, at an early age.

Now we come to the difficult aspect of their personality, or at least their personality as it really should be. You will recall that the Breed Standard requires the Lhasa Apso to be 'aloof with strangers'. In fact the word 'aloof' was substituted for the word 'chary' when the Standard was rewritten in 1984, for it was felt that there was a danger of breeders misinterpreting the original word to mean 'shy'. Without going into the ins and outs of the various ways these words can or cannot be interpreted, suffice it to say that it is in the Apso's nature to be a little cautious of strangers. That is not to say that he is frightened of them but that he wishes to make up his own mind as to whether or not they are worthy of his attentions. Some Apsos will indeed bounce up to every individual who calls at your door if they are brought up to do so, but do not necessarily expect this of your little companion for, in reality, this is not his true nature. In some of the very interesting discussions I have had with Tibetans about the Apso in its mother-land, it is clear that the breed can be quite aggressive with strangers. Clearly, it is certainly not expected that a stranger can go up to one and pet it without preliminary introduction by its owner. Think back to the Apso's ancestors in Tibet: they were watchdogs and were expected to give a warning bark when strangers approached. Keep the dog's ancestry in the back of your mind at all times and you will understand more easily what goes on in his mind.

How Much Exercise Does He Need?

As an active dog with short legs he will take as much or as little exercise as you will give him, but clearly, if he is a single pet he should be taken out for interesting walks and be given some free run if possible, for he will not have had the opportunity to expend his energies with canine companions. It is quite surprising how much exercise dogs give each other when playing together, for they twist and turn their bodies in play using all their muscles as they do so. A fit Lhasa Apso can often comfortably out-walk one of the large breeds – those little legs just have to go twice as fast to keep up with the bigger dog's pace!

Every person's domestic arrangements are different but I would say that an Apso could live in virtually any home. Even a flat can be suitable provided that, in this case, he is taken on frequent walks. Whether he is owned by the fit and active or the not-so-active he must have some sort of exercise or, like any dog, he will quickly become overweight and lethargic. Remember that his mind needs exercise as well as his body and a walk or exercise outdoors will give him fresh smells and new things to think about. One word of warning though: if your Apso is kept in full coat his hair will sweep up bits of debris, and any such twigs or little pieces of bracken etc. must be removed immediately upon returning home if they are not to mat the coat.

How Prone is He to Illness?

A Lhasa Apso is no more prone to illness than any other dog and certainly he is generally fitter than a good many breeds. Naturally, your dog's health will depend largely on how well you care for him but all dogs succumb to ailments of some kind from time to time. You will find a section on illness later in this book but it is fair to say that if you have bought a well-reared puppy, fed him regularly with sensible food and have generally cared for him properly you should not encounter any major health problems. Having said that, any dog can be unfortunate enough to pick up a virus but if your dog is kept in tip-top condition his tough little body will do its utmost to fight it off.

Lifespan

The majority of Apsos live into their early teens. Sixteen-year-olds are not infrequent and there have been reports of just a few making it into their early twenties.

Whereas an eight- or nine-year-old member of a larger breed will be well past its prime, an Apso of a similar age can still be almost as sprightly as a puppy.

Care of the ageing dog is dealt with fully later in the book.

Is He Noisy?

A Lhasa Apso cannot be expected not to bark for, after all, his main purpose in the monasteries of his home country was to give a warning bark. He will, however, usually bark only at the approach of visitors and, once they have been welcomed and accepted by you, his owner, he will quieten without further ado. Although I doubt any of us feel that barking is a particularly pleasant sound, the Apso's bark is not shrill but rather mellow. Often, if unseen, he will sound like a substantially larger dog.

Without doubt kennelled dogs tend to bark more frequently than those kept in the house but I feel sure this is true of most breeds. It does not necessarily mean that they are any less happy but they seem to enjoy communicating with one another from some distance! It is interesting to note that Apsos are quite capable of howling. Most people who keep just Apsos do not find that they howl in the true sense of the word, but keeping hounds as I do, I find that if the hounds set up a howl the Apsos readily join in with varying degrees of pitch and melodious harmony. One dog learns from another and it is not always the hounds who begin the chorus! Personally I adore the sound and I find that this strange melody is a constant source of amusement to visitors. I have not yet worked out quite why the 'singing' always stops so abruptly, as if the chorus master had 'cued them out' in unison.

Cleanliness in the House

Whilst it is usually more difficult to house-train an older dog, house-training a youngster should present no major problems but, again, we shall deal with this aspect more thoroughly later on. There is a tendency for people to feel that bitches are perhaps cleaner than dogs but, unless a dog has been used at stud, both sexes should be clean in the house if trained correctly from the outset and providing, of course, they have no kidney or bladder problems due to infirmity.

Will He Shed His Coat?

Certainly the Apso will not shed a great amount of coat; indeed the very fact that he does not is one of the reasons why the coat mats and therefore needs regular grooming. Coat will be removed during grooming sessions and it is usually wise to have a special area of the home set aside for grooming, for loose hair can easily fly about, especially whilst using a hairdryer.

However, as little coat is lost other than when being groomed, the breed is more suitable than most for people with allergies – although no one who suffers from an allergy should rush out to buy an Apso unless they have at least experimented with the breed around them in a confined space.

Will He Climb?

Just occasionally you may be unlucky enough to get a 'climber'. The first time your Apso is found in the garden rather than in the run, you imagine it must have escaped without notice when you closed the gate. After checking the gate to see that it cannot have pushed underneath, you deposit your Apso back in the run, perplexed. You have been fooled. Soon after, the same Apso is discovered out again and when this has happened two or three times you realise that the only way out is over! It is not easy to catch an Apso in the act but to do so is an amazing sight, one you almost cannot believe. A 'climber' (and thankfully there are not too many of them) can scale 3 ft (90 cm) fences and even 6 ft (180 cm) fences, so, if such a fate befalls you, you will have to engineer a method of putting some sort of ridge (preferably rounded, and not wide enough for the dog to balance on) part of the way up the inside of the run. This seems to beat the guilty Apso at his own game – but always bear in mind that if it has happened once it can happen again. Exercise caution at all times!

How Well Will He React to Children?

Where children are concerned, so very much depends upon the children themselves and how carefully they are supervised by their parents. For these reasons it is always difficult to give advice on this aspect but if an Apso is handled gently by a child it should respond by being equally gentle. Any dog which is ill-treated (albeit unwittingly) by a child will defend itself in the only way it knows how and could, of course, cause injury by doing so.

From a purely personal point of view I am reluctant to sell puppies to homes with very young children unless I know the parents to be ultra-sensible with both children and dogs. Having said that, after very careful appraisal of the circumstances, I have placed puppies in homes with children and have often found that children and dogs have formed the very closest of bonds.

Will He be Travel-Sick?

This may sound a silly question, but it is so terribly important, for a sickly dog can completely ruin Sunday's drive out. Worse still, if the dog is persistently sick the temptation is to leave it at home and thus it spends many more hours alone than it would otherwise do.

In a word, 'yes' it may be sick, but, equally, it may well not be. Thankfully, for those who suffer in this way (and this of course applies to any breed of dog) there are some excellent proprietary brands of travel-sickness tablets available from most good pet shops. Some come in two strengths: a small tablet for puppies and a larger one for adults. Be sure to read the instructions carefully and you will avoid some very unpleasant journeys.

If you do find that your young puppy travels badly it is a good idea to take him out in the car for several short journeys. Don't avoid the car, for you will only be putting off the problem until another day. It is also helpful if he can be kept in a confined space; if he is at liberty to roam around, for example, in the back of an estate car, his tummy seems to get more upset. Don't think he won't grow out of it for he most probably will. Once he has had a few comfortable journeys with the aid of a tablet you should be able to wean him off them and, in most cases, you will find that his old problems are unlikely to recur.

You may have heard it said that human travel-sickness tablets will do the trick just as well. Perhaps they do, but one has to be very careful about overdosing. In recent years canine tablets have been much more easily available so I recommend that you use a remedy which has been designed especially for dogs.

SELECTION OF A PUPPY

If you have decided that a Lhasa Apso is the breed for you, how do you go about obtaining one? Apsos may be advertised in local newspapers but, especially if you are new to the breed, you cannot know that they are from good stock or that they have been well reared. The fact that they have a pedigree and have perhaps been registered with the Kennel Club does not guarantee that the puppies offered for sale are typical specimens of the breed.

The very fact that you have become interested in the breed may mean that you have friends with Apsos and it will be natural to make enquiries through them as to the breeders of their own dogs and whether they would recommend that you contact them. If this course of action is not open to you (and even if it is) you would be well advised to attend one of the many Championship shows which are held up and down the country throughout the year. Watch the dogs from the ringside, learn as much as possible by talking to exhibitors around the ring and you may begin to form some opinion of the breeding you would most like to have. You will, with the aid of a catalogue which lists all the exhibitors, discover which breeders live relatively near to you, although to get the dog you want you should be prepared to travel.

If you cannot manage to get to a show, details of breeders can be obtained from directories and from the *Kennel Gazette*, which is published monthly and available from the Kennel Club. There are also two weekly canine newspapers (*Our Dogs* and *Dog World*) in which advertisements can usually be found. The Secretaries of the three Lhasa Apso clubs may also be able to help you locate suitable breeders in your area. I have given current contact addresses at the back of this book and the Kennel Club should be able to provide up-to-date details of how to get in touch with them.

Show or Pet?

I mentioned earlier that you should be prepared to travel to get the dog you want; you may also have to wait, particularly if you want to acquire a specimen which may be worthy of the show ring.

Very many people want a Lhasa Apso just as a companion, a four-legged friend simply to share the comforts of their home; such owners may be clear from the start that they are never likely to have any intention of exhibiting a dog; nevertheless, if genuinely interested in the breed, they will want to be sure that they obtain a typical specimen which has been reared with just as much care and attention as a potential show dog. There are others who are lured by the idea of exhibiting and feel they would like to obtain a puppy which is likely to be suitable to take to shows; indeed they may already be owners of a pet Apso and now feel that they would like to show the breed if they could manage to obtain a dog of show quality.

Yet another category of prospective owners are those who have already been bitten by the show bug, perhaps in another breed, and they know from the outset that they want to obtain the very best specimen available to them.

It is of paramount importance that the prospective owner makes perfectly clear his possible requirements when speaking to breeders for no breeder worth her salt will try to sell a pet quality dog to a show home – such folly will do the breeder's reputation no end of harm for it is to her advantage to have the very best representatives of her kennel exhibited at shows. On the other hand, it is unfair of a prospective owner to doggedly insist that he must have the very best puppy in the litter when he knows that he has no intention of exhibiting it.

But there can always be exceptions. Occasionally one hears stories of the breeder who sold a dog as a pet, and when for some reason it was returned to the breeder he recognised its virtues, campaigned it and went on to make it a champion. Such things do happen, but not with any great frequency. Puppies change so very much as they grow older and it is simply not possible for a breeder to be sure that a particular dog will end up as a winning specimen of the breed. Indeed the breeder, if she knows her own breeding well, has a reasonably good idea from a very early age but unseen faults can develop long after the puppy has left its breeder.

It can be equally annoying, by the way, if a dog has been sold as a pet (but with full documentation) and the new owner decides, after all, to put the dog in the show ring. Such action by the new owner is unlikely to curry favour with the breeder unless this has been fully discussed beforehand and the dog's merits assessed. It may well be that a dog is of good enough quality to be entered at smaller shows for a little fun but is unlikely to be placed highly at Championship events; in such a case the breeder would doubtless prefer the owner not to enter the latter events and certainly not the most highly competitive classes!

What to Look For in a Healthy Puppy

The puppy you eventually choose should be lively and bright. Do not be tempted to feel sorry for the nervous little one which scuttles away and hides in a corner. Certainly you should keep in mind the rather special temperament of the breed and take that into account, but none the less puppies should be happy and playful at such a young age. You will, however, perhaps like also to bear in mind the fact that the puppy may not have been in the breeder's sitting room before and this can account for a certain amount of insecurity, for the puppy's environment is initially new to him.

You must expect your prospective puppy to be clean; that is to say his coat should look clean and be free from stickiness, especially around the eyes and back end. If the breeder has brought up the litter with due care and attention it is only natural that she will want the puppies to look their very best when being presented to likely purchasers. It is usually possible to assess from the puppies' presentation something of the way in which they have been brought up. It goes without saying that the puppies should have no signs of fleas or other parasites and the insides of the ears should, of course, be clean.

A charming litter of young Belazieth puppies.

If you are offered for sale an Apso puppy of anything less then eight weeks of age, take special care. Some breeders do sell at the age of seven weeks but, personally, I consider this too young. Without doubt, breeders of puppies which are sold at six weeks or younger should be given a very wide berth. If it is your intention to purchase a dog for the show ring, the older the puppy, the more chance you will have of assessing its merits. Some of those breeders who have stock for sale which they believe to have show potential will 'run on' the puppy for a few weeks until they have a clearer idea of how it is likely to develop. The eventual number and positioning of the teeth can often be very difficult to assess in a young Apso for the jaw can continue to move until the dog is adult and, unfortunately, a full first set of teeth is no sure guarantee that the second set will be equally correct.

Sometimes a breeder may offer for sale a bitch puppy with special conditions known as 'breeding terms'. These can vary considerably but are perhaps most likely to involve the purchaser in being committed to breed from the bitch by a certain age and to let the original bitch's breeder have one or two puppies of his or her choosing. Breeding terms can be tricky so be sure that if you do get involved in a contract of this nature the terms are set down in black and white so that each party knows exactly what the agreement is. Provisions should be made to cover the eventuality that the bitch is not capable of breeding; and be sure you know whether the breeder is to have first pick or, for example, first and second or first and third. It is heartbreaking for owners of their first litter to become attached to one puppy which has become special to them, only to find that the bitch's breeder chooses that very one and the enthusiastic new breeders can do nothing about it if they are to keep to the terms of the agreement. Always remember that because one is excited about buying one's original stock it is very easy to misunderstand what is being said, and it is equally easy for words which have never been committed to paper to change in both parties' minds as years progress. In such arrangements it is the breeder of the bitch who sets down the terms and he or she may ask for one or more puppies to be returned in due course.

Special terms can also, occasionally, be set down for dogs, giving, for example, the original breeder the right to use the dog at stud on a specified or unlimited number of the breeder's own bitches. Purchasers of puppies intended only as pets should think very carefully before entering into any such agreements for they may not wish to breed and a stud dog is not likely to be the cleanest pet around the home.

PUPPY CARE

If you wish to set your own mind at rest as to whether the puppy you have purchased is healthy, you can take it immediately to a vet to have it checked over. For those who do not already have a vet this can be a good introduction. It is always worth bearing in mind, however, that this particular vet may not be familiar with Lhasa Apsos. Do not let him tell you that the bite is incorrect because it is reverse scissor!

The age at which you bought your puppy will determine whether or not the puppy has already had any of its vaccinations or whether it is due to have them almost immediately. Vaccinations are being updated all the time and different vets use vaccines from varying suppliers. For this reason you really must take the advice of the vet as to the precise age at which the puppy should have his jabs, dependent upon which vaccine he uses in his practice. Do, however, be certain that your puppy has the full course of treatment and that the vaccination programme includes some measure of protection against Parvovirus. When you collect your puppy from the breeder be sure to ask whether the puppy has been injected at all and, if so, obtain written evidence showing which vaccines have been used. Do, by the way, remember, that when you take your unvaccinated puppy to the veterinary surgery he should not be allowed to come into contact with other dogs, nor with chair seats and certainly not with the floor! A Lhasa Apso is quite small enough to remain in your arms, however long the queue in the waiting room. And discourage those friendly people who want to come and look at the sweet little thing and poke their fingers at him – you don't know with what those fingers have been in contact! You will have plenty of opportunity to show off your newly acquired companion after his vaccination programme is complete. I know it seems a long wait, but that wait is well worthwhile.

Hopefully your puppy's breeder will have wormed the litter and will have given you precise instructions as to the remainder of the worming programme, possibly having given you a suitable tablet, maybe even cut into appropriate portions. If no tablets have been provided you would be well advised to obtain your supply from the vet for those sold over the counter in pet shops are not generally so effective. Take care to give the correct amount of tablet at each worming session and be sure that the tablet does eventually disappear down the throat rather than into the depths of the dog's chin furnishings. Some Apsos have a canny habit of pretending to have swallowed the intended item, only to spit it out, usually sideways, some minutes later. When the tablet seems to have gone down, hold the jaw closed until the dog swallows and, hopefully, you will have achieved your aim.

Coat Care for the Young Puppy

If you abide by the maxim that you can never begin too soon, both you and your puppy will grow to enjoy the grooming sessions which are to become such an important part of the dog's adult life. Within the first few days of obtaining your puppy gently go through his coat with a soft brush or even a wide-toothed comb, just to get him used to the feel of grooming equipment. You should try even from the very early stages to roll him over on to his side or on to his back, still gently grooming. If you can get him used to this now, whilst his coat is still short and the brush or comb unlikely to encounter knots which hurt, you will find his adult coat much easier to deal with. Make grooming a pleasure from the start and it will continue to be so.

Practise, too, looking inside his ears, for as he grows up hair will grow inside the ears and this will need to be removed. Unless you have a particularly heavily coated puppy you may not need to remove any of the hair from inside the ear within the first few weeks but it is a good idea to get the puppy used to having you lift the ear flap so that he does not resist too strongly when the time comes. This, by the way, is best done whilst he is lying on his side.

Keep an eye out for dirty bottoms for a puppy who moves to a new home is more susceptible to upset tummies than one who remains with his breeder. Even if your puppy's motions remain entirely normal, he can still very easily get tacky around that area and if not noticed soon enough he can quickly get a very uncomfortable and often very sore bottom. Unpleasant though the subject may be, if you have chosen to have a long-coated breed you must be prepared to cope with the less appealing aspects too. I find that the easiest way to deal with a youngster's dirty bottom is to literally sit him on the edge of the bathroom sink so that you can grip him firmly with your left arm (assuming that you are right-handed) whilst you clean up the problem with your right. He must be made to feel safe in your arms and the water must not be too hot, for his young skin will be tender. Soon the task will be over and he will be grateful to you for having sorted out his little problem. Don't forget to dry him off before he goes back on the floor; a quick dab with loo roll or kitchen towelling takes off a good deal of the moisture before you use his own towel.

Keep an eye on the length of his claws for in the very early stages of his life he is less likely to walk regularly on hard surfaces which will naturally wear them down. If he has not had his dew claws removed these will have to be checked regularly throughout his life for they will never wear down of their own accord. In the very young puppy claws can be trimmed with ordinary human nail scissors. If the claws are pale in colour it is possible to see where the blood vessels end and, naturally, you trim well clear of them. In dogs with darker-coloured claws extreme care must be taken not to cut into the vessels, so always cut too little rather than too much, even if it involves several short snippings.

The young puppy's coat will not yet be long enough for knots to form between his pads but, whilst you have him lying on his side, check carefully between the pads to get him used to the procedure. At this stage you can also practise snipping away just a fraction of the coat around the edges of his feet to keep them tidy and to get him used to this for when he is older and in full coat. Practice makes perfect, and the more trouble you take in the puppy's first few months of life, the easier his grooming sessions will be for both of you when he is mature.

Eyes will need to be kept clean from the minute the puppy becomes yours. Lhasa Apsos do not normally get excessively dirty eyes but there is often a small amount of discharge in the inner corner of the eye. The inexperienced may feel that the kindest way of dealing with this is to dab away tentatively with a moist piece of cotton wool; this, however, is *not* the way to deal with an Apso's eyes for, as someone once said to me, 'I spend half an hour a day dabbing his eyes and they're still never right!' Be firm with your puppy and, using extreme care, take a small, fine-toothed comb from the inner corner of the eye outwards; you will find that the comb takes any discharge away with it and the puppy feels no discomfort. Having said that, if the eye is allowed to become too sticky before you do this you would be wiser to moisten the area and remove the bulk of the matter with your fingers before applying the comb. Lastly, do not, under any circumstances, be tempted to trim the puppy's beautiful long eyelashes. The breed has long eyelashes for a very specific purpose: to keep the long adult coat from falling into the eyes. Something we must not be tempted to do is to interfere with nature any more than necessary!

Getting Used to the Lead

At the first contact with a collar and lead you will very probably have a rebellion on your hands. The pretty little collar you have chosen may look perfectly harmless to you but you will be surprised how much your canine companion is going to detest it! Some take to it better than others but it is always wisest to be prepared for the worst.

I suggest that you first of all practise with just a collar. Choose one which is very light and, ideally, slips over the head of the puppy so that you do not have to mess about unnecessarily with fastenings. Be sure that it is not so large that it dangles and gets caught on objects around the home if the puppy is out of your sight for a moment or two. Not everyone perhaps shares my opinion but I feel it is wise to put a collar around the neck when the puppy is very young. If you have bought your puppy rather than bred it you could begin about a week after you have it, just as soon as you feel he has settled in well. Your beloved puppy will not hate you for ever. He may scream and run away from you at first, and will surely try to scratch away to remove this very unpleasant contraption, but if you leave it on for just a few minutes at a time and try to distract his attention from it he will soon overcome his fears. Practise, as I have said, for just a few minutes once or twice a day and stay with him, for he will need reassurance and you must take care that he does not become entangled in any way.

Eventually, when he is fairly confident about wearing his collar, you can introduce the lead – again just a lightweight one and preferably one which can be attached to his new collar. Remember that your puppy has never been restrained in this way; he has always walked in the direction of his choosing and it will doubtless go against the grain to be forced in another direction. This part of his training is just as strange to him as the feel of a collar around his neck.

A few minutes a day is enough. Start by putting the puppy on the ground and calling him to you whilst you hold the end of the lead. This will not pull and, to begin with, he will probably not realise that he is attached to anything at all. I then like to let the puppy take me, allowing him to go in his own direction whilst I follow behind; again, he is scarcely aware that I am doing anything other than walking near to him. As his confidence grows and as he becomes more and more aware that he is not entirely free, start to guide him a little, tugging firmly but gently when necessary.

Every dog reacts slightly differently and it takes a lot of patience on both parts. Don't let him get the better of you, make sure he knows that you are the boss and, slowly but surely, you will win in the end. Try, though, to understand his obvious reluctance for in this way you will both have more respect for each other.

Naturally, this training must be done initially in his own surroundings where he is completely out of harm's way. There should be no distractions at first; no children playing around him, desperate to 'have a go' too; and no other pets around with whom he would prefer to frolic. Lead training is a serious business; your puppy will need your undivided attention, firmness and a kind word to encourage him when he succeeds in pleasing you. Some puppies apparently take to lead training like a duck does to water – they must be very few!

Stages of Growing Up

The most outward sign of your Apso's development from puppyhood to adulthood is displayed in his coat change. Different lines of breeding develop more or less slowly; sometimes a puppy has a very full coat by the age of six or seven months, but in others the coat is not at its fullest until the age of about ten months. However quickly your puppy's coat develops, one thing you can be sure of is that it will, eventually, go through a very substantial change from puppy coat to adult coat. The often somewhat fluffy coat will shed and in its place will grow a coat of a different texture. If the coat is of good quality, this will be hard with a dense but softer undercoat.

The time at which this change takes place also varies according to the puppy's breeding but coat change usually happens between the ages of about ten and eighteen months. This is a time when the coat needs a great deal of attention. Because the puppy coat is shedding, the hair can mat very easily so it is wise to groom a little more regularly than usual. The dead hair really does need to come out to make way for the new growth but, on the other hand, if one takes out too much dead coat one can be left with a very sparsely coated Apso. Now is the time when you may find it beneficial to give some sort of food supplement to help give strength and body to the new coat.

Modhish Miss Fandango pictured at 10 months.

At this age your Apso is not only undergoing physical changes but mental ones too; the dog is maturing sexually and is often somewhat sensitive about his private parts. Please also bear in mind that Lhasa Apso males are often perfectly capable of mating a bitch at the age of eight months (or even less!). I am not here suggesting that they should mate a bitch so young but that every caution should be taken if bitches are in season around them.

An Apso bitch will usually come into season somewhere between the ages of six and nine months but there are, as in any breed, always exceptions to the rule. To cite an example, one of my own bitches first came into season at the tender age of only five months and then surprised everyone by having another season at nine months, following which she fell into a regular six-monthly pattern. One does, however, frequently find that bitches' seasons are not as regular as one might wish and I would certainly recommend that one seeks veterinary advice if the gap between seasons is over-long.

After her first season a bitch's personality will sometimes change somewhat: she may simply appear to be much more mature or, conversely, may be rather 'scatty' as a result of this bodily change. Personally I feel that during this period of change neither dogs nor bitches should be subjected to any undue stress or to any unnecessary change in their environment. It is my belief that they need your support at this stage in their development, almost more than at any other time.

> Which end is which of an Apso?
> They're identical, so it appears.
> I am told mine's a bitch,
> but I wish I knew which
> end to search for her eyes and her ears.
>
> P.S. I've just found a solution
> which strikes me as fool-proof and neat –
> besides being no bother
> to one end (or other) –
> just offer a plateful of meat.

> by The Hon. Mrs E. A. Watson
> (owner of Brackenbury Yang-Si)

6 Coat Care and Grooming in Adulthood

Naturally, if you wish to keep your Apso in full coat it will involve a fair amount of grooming on a regular basis. Before we consider how best to approach this task let us look once again at the coat of the dog as it was kept in Tibet.

We have already said that if the coat is of correct texture in maturity there will be a dense undercoat and a longer top coat of harder texture, usually with each strand being very much thicker than that of the coat underneath. The Apso developed this coat as a protection from the cold climate, but, perhaps surprisingly, the density of coat also acts as an insulation against the heat. Nevertheless, at least in some areas of Tibet, we understand that the coat was shorn in summer so that it could be used to make clothing. You may notice, however, that the Apso grows a slightly thicker undercoat in winter than it does in summer, hence a dog kept in centrally heated conditions will not usually have such a profuse coat as one which is exposed to the elements throughout the year.

Although the Apso is a long-coated breed, in the dog's original environment it would have been a rare sight indeed to see its coat sweeping the ground such as we see in the show ring today. Because the Apso does not shed its coat in the way that most breeds do, the dead coat automatically becomes entangled with the rest of the coat and forms mats. Only grooming will remove this dead hair.

As the years have progressed we seem to have bred for more and more profuse coats and many people, particularly in recent years, have expressed some concern for the Apso's ability to see well enough with its long hair falling over its eyes. Again, I think it does us good to recall why the hair was so.

If you look carefully at your Apso's eyes you will see that the eyelashes are of quite extraordinary length in proportion to the size of the dog. These long eyelashes in fact prevent the hair from falling into the eyes and, left to fall naturally, the coat forms a kind of curtain which shields the eyes from extremely strong light. Anyone who has travelled to Tibet will tell you of the immense clarity of vision and the brightness of light due to the rarefied atmosphere. Added to this, if the skull shape of the Apso is typical of the breed, the head furnishings will not fall completely down over the entire front of the forehead but will, of their own accord, fall very slightly to the sides.

People attracted to the Lhasa Apso are, almost inevitably, attracted also to the breed's profuse coat. Indeed a mature Apso in full show coat is a very splendid sight. Even if one does not wish to show one's Apso it is of course quite possible to keep the dog in full coat, but there is no disgrace in choosing to keep the coat shorter if you wish. After all, there is much more to love about the Apso than simply his coat! An Apso which is kept clean and comfortable in short coat is much happier, and often healthier, than one which is full of mats and tangles. Before we even talk about grooming, let me say now that if ever circumstances such as, for example, hospitalisation prevent you from keeping your pet's long coat in good condition it is much wiser to have it clipped off, perhaps at a dog grooming parlour. And don't be embarrassed about taking it to a parlour if it already has more knots than it should; people who groom professionally are quite used to this. Think of the dog, not of your pride. Just bear in mind that the coat will grow again, albeit quite slowly, so when circumstances permit, your Apso can be allowed to return to his former glory! Always remember that a badly matted coat can conceal all sorts of problems: not only does the dog smell and possibly harbour fleas, but also it will have trouble with its toilet and can quite easily develop sore patches on its skin which, if they go undetected, can become most unpleasant.

Although I have absolutely no wish to deter you from owning an Apso I believe it is only fair to the dog to point out the problems which can so easily occur, resulting in distressed dogs and owners. So let us start as we mean to go on, by learning how to deal with the coat so that it does *not* become a problem!

We have already said that if you start training your puppy from an early age it will grow to enjoy grooming sessions and grooming will be a pleasure for both dog and owner. Time spent grooming your dog is time spent *with* him and it is surprising how much one establishes a rapport with one's beloved four-legged companion when he is on the grooming table. It is a time for talking to him; tell him all your news, to pour out your heart to him if you wish – he'll listen if no one else will! He will enjoy having you talk to him so don't be silent, but, on the other hand, remember that you also need to be firm, never forgetting for one minute that *you* are the boss.

I shall not endeavour to give hard and fast rules about exactly which is the best way to groom, for those of us who show our dogs all use slightly different techniques. You will discover that you develop your own in time. You may well find that the frequency with which you need to bath your dog varies according to the texture of the dog's coat and the circumstances in which your dog is kept. Some people like to bath the night prior to a show; others prefer to do so one or two days before, so that the coat has time to 'settle' before the day of the show. I know of one successful exhibitor who only baths legs, tummy and head furnishings before a show and apparently gives a full bath only two or three times a year. She feels this is the best way to retain the coat's natural oils.

Indeed there are a few others who never bath their dogs at all but clearly they groom thoroughly and frequently so that they, also, can show their dogs in full and glamorous coat.

From a purely personal point of view I like to bath my dogs the day before a show, although some black dogs I find are better done a day or two before, if, of course, one can manage to keep them clean until show day! So much depends upon the dog's environment, whether it is kept in the house or in an outside kennel and whether or not its exercise area is covered. If a beautifully groomed dog runs on grass and chooses to stand out in the pouring rain (believe me, some do), it's probably simplest to start all over again!

When prospective pet owners see a splendidly coated show dog, often their first question is 'How long did it take you to get him looking like that?' In a nutshell, and as a *very* general guide, a dog in full coat and with not too many knots from the outset, takes about two hours for a full bath and groom (with the right equipment). Between baths it is essential to spend a little extra time grooming your dog to keep him free from major tangles.

I mention the 'right equipment'. It is unlikely that you will want to spend a fortune on a professional dog hairdryer if you have only one or perhaps two pets but, that aside, let us look at what you will need.

Essentials

COMBS A medium-/wide-toothed comb and a small comb with narrow teeth.

BRUSH Preferably of pure bristle in a soft cushioning.

SHAMPOO There is a wide variety of canine shampoos on the market and you should choose one which will not make the coat too soft. A standard insecticidal shampoo is suitable for most coats and there is the added benefit that it will act as a deterrent to any stray flea which happens to come into the vicinity of your own precious Apso. (By the way, such shampoos will not leave your dog with that distinctive overpowering odour associated with flea sprays.)

SCISSORS A good sharp pair of hairdressing scissors, kept specifically for the purpose.

TABLE The table on which you groom needs to be waist-high and with a non-slippery surface. If you use one of the tables in your home you would be well advised to purchase a fairly large-sized rubber car mat to put on the table. A variety of dog-grooming tables can be purchased, many of which are collapsible and fitted with wheels so that they double up as a trolley for taking to shows. Such tables are by no means inexpensive but can give you several years of good service.

NAIL CLIPPERS Unless you are always going to have your dog's claws clipped by a vet or a grooming parlour you will need at least to have access to a pair of nail clippers. There are two types: guillotine and staight-edged; which you choose to use is very much a matter of preference.

EAR TWEEZERS These are to be used with extreme care but I consider them an essential item as hair constantly grows inside the ears of the Apso and in the majority of cases is best removed with certain frequency. The tweezers must be of good quality and blunt-ended to minimise the risk of mishap.

TOWELS You will need at least one good-sized towel in which to wrap your dog when he comes out of the bath and a couple of small ones for everyday use on wet feet.

Helpful extras

COAT CONDITIONER To make grooming easier and to prevent the hair from splitting it is sensible to apply a conditioning rinse after shampooing your dog. Again, choose one which is not specifically designed to soften the coat – you simply want to use it to help groom out tangles and prevent the ends of the coat being broken off unnecessarily.

BABY SHAMPOO Some owners prefer to use a mild baby shampoo for the whiskers and beard.

ELASTICS 'Dental elastics' are tiny, cream-coloured, elastic bands which are frequently used to tie up the dog's head furnishings to prevent breakage and soiling of the coat when eating and drinking. If you do choose to take your dog's hair away from its face in this way (which is not essential), be sure to cut out the elastics, never pull or you will undo all the good you may otherwise have done. Small hair slides may be used as an alternative and some owners make little crocheted 'hats' designed specifically to suit the Apso's head furnishings.

METAL PIN BRUSH You may like to 'finish' the coat with a metal pin brush but never attempt to use one for the full grooming process or you will take out too much coat. (Alternatively a good finish can be obtained with your medium-/wide-toothed comb.)

CONDITIONING SPRAY With the recently introduced and rather nebulous Kennel Club rule about not altering the texture of the coat, I leave it to the reader to decide which conditioning sprays are or are not permissible for use in the show ring. Suffice it to say that for many years it has been common practice to use a spray conditioner upon completion of grooming in order to prevent static and to give some protection to the ends of the coat, especially if the dog's coat has to come into contact with a rough surface such as concrete.

A Tip Or Two Before You Start Grooming

- Give your dog ample opportunity to relieve himself before the grooming session begins or you could have an unnecessarily restless (and uncomfortable) dog on the table.
- Never leave your dog on the table unattended – he could so easily decide to jump off and, in doing so, hurt a limb or break a tooth or, worse still, both!
- Never groom the coat whilst it is absolutely dry or you will break the ends and very probably take out far more coat than you originally intended. Always use a water or conditioning spray even if your dog will very soon end up in the bath.

NOTE: Some people prefer to groom out thoroughly before bathing whilst others, myself included, groom out whilst drying.

Start As You Mean To Go On

As I said earlier, if grooming is to be a pleasure to all parties concerned you must be in total control of the dog. You will be more likely to groom successfully if you can train your dog to lie on his side, for in this way can you get in every little nook and cranny.

So begin by teaching the dog to lie over on his side. Grasp firmly, but not too tightly, at the top of the legs farthest away from you and gently roll him over so that his four feet are facing you. This may sound difficult but it really is not and a well-trained dog will more or less carry out the procedure himself. As he goes over keep your body close to his, leaning over him slightly yourself. Talk to him to calm him and, in the early stages, it may help to gently stroke his side until he relaxes fully. (Some of our 'old hands' love it so much that they fall fast asleep and the difficulty is making them stand up again!)

It is not unusual for your dog to attempt to struggle at first but he should be commanded with a firm 'No', or perhaps 'Down', and you should press firmly (but never too heavily) on his shoulders and back end so that he knows exactly where you want him to stay.

Spray the coat lightly, if not already wet from the bath, and commence grooming from a certain point so that you know exactly which areas you've done. Perhaps the best place to start is on the stomach, parting the hair as you go along so that no tiny tangle escapes you, and working up the side of the body. Brush the hair fairly gently and if you find knots which will not readily brush out, tease them out with your fingers or with the end of your comb, always parting the knot from the inside out, *never* the other way round. If a mat is particularly large (and sometimes large knots can appear virtually overnight, especially during the change from puppy to adult coat), divide in into two or three sections and work on each smaller section in turn. Never tug, always tease and then brush through when the knot has disappeared.

Pay special attention to knots which have formed in the groin, under the front 'arm-pits' and behind the ears, for these are the areas which seem to be most prone to tangles. Do also take care when combing around nipples and remember that dogs have nipples too, not just bitches!

Whilst still in the 'nether regions', if you have a male Apso you will need to trim the long hair which grows from the tip of the penis. However, always leave a good $\frac{1}{2}$ inch (12 mm) of hair, never less, or the short hairs can irritate and even set up a little infection. Groom carefully around the anus and you will find that there is, quite simply, absolutely no need to trim around it, provided that it is kept clean and tangle free at all times.

It is wise to tackle the legs next, ideally starting from the thigh and working downwards towards the toes. You will very probably find that your Apso is particularly sensitive about grooming in and around his toes so seek out with great care any little knots which have formed on the top of the foot, between the toes. At this stage don't worry about the underneath of the foot – we shall come to that later.

Now begin work in the same way under the chin and on the head, whiskers, beard and ears. You will have to groom very carefully in this area to avoid accidentally catching the eye or lips. You are also likely to find that the face is a little tacky from feeding and that there has been a little discharge from the eyes, so do take care not to tug at the coat for this can be uncomfortable and painful for the dog. You will find your fine-toothed comb helpful in removing matter around the muzzle. Start below the eye and move the comb downwards and outwards. Do try to keep the facial area clear on a regular basis for if left for a few days any discharge from the eyes will build up and cause a slight odour, as well as being very unpleasant for the dog. When combing through the hair on the ear be sure to remember that the skin of the ear (the leather) can be easily damaged and the ends of the coat can break very readily.

Finally move to the tail (some may, however, prefer to do the tail before the head). Always work from the root of the tail outwards but if removing tangles it is not wise to take the comb right through to the ends of the coat if one is to avoid splitting the hair. Any damaged ends will be seen particularly easily on the tail.

The Finishing Touches

REMOVING HAIR FROM INSIDE THE EARS Whilst your dog is lying on his side you should lift the ear flap and check that there has been no build-up of hair or wax inside the ear canal. Never probe into the ear but if hair does need to be removed use the tweezers with utmost care. Grasp the ends of a few hairs together and pull steadily away, following the direction in which the hair is growing. Surprisingly, and providing that you are careful, this will not cause the dog any discomfort for the ear canal is less sensitive than many other areas of the body.

UNDER THE PADS Carefully inspect between the pads of each foot to check for any build-up of coat which has matted. This is not always easy to see and, if left, will solidify into a very hard ball, causing great discomfort when pressure is placed on the foot. It goes without saying that you will have to be very careful in cutting out any knots here, so try never to let them form.

The hair is capable of growing quite long underneath the foot so you will need to trim this off roughly once every one or two weeks.

THE PARTING Now, at last, your dog can stand whilst you make a parting, working with the end of the comb, from nose to tail. Gently comb through with the wide section of your larger comb (or your metal pin-brush if you prefer) to see the finished result.

TRIMMING THE ENDS If your dog has a particularly long coat you may decide to trim very slightly at 'floor level'. The Lhasa Apso is *not* a trimmed breed so any adjustments you make to the length of the coat should look as natural as possible. Nothing looks worse than a dead straight line cut half an inch above the ground! There are, however, good reasons for slight trimming, for a dog with excessive coat can trip up by actually walking on the front of the coat if it is too long. I must stress, however, that you must be careful not to spoil the coat by trimming. It would be such a pity to ruin that lovely coat (which seemed to take an eternity to grow) merely with a slip of the scissors!

Bathing

If your bath has a slippery surface it will be helpful to place a rubber mat in the bath to help your dog to feel secure. He should also be trained to stand where you put him; you do not want him constantly wandering from one end of the bath to the other, or scrambling up the sides.

A shower attachment is a virtual necessity and you should not put the plug in the bath for you will want the water to flow away freely. The water should be neither too hot nor too cold, and do be sure to test if *before* your introduce your four-legged companion to it. By the way, many male dogs seem, understandably, to be very particular about the temperature of the water on their testicles, so do take extreme care in that general area.

If the dog is bathed frequently you may not always need to apply the shampoo twice – once is often enough – but most importantly you must *never* rub the shampoo into the coat or you will create knots. Just stroke or squeeze the shampoo into the coat and be sure to rinse out *very* thoroughly. Any conditioner used should be applied in the same way, left in the coat for a moment or two (or as directed) and rinsed out well.

Try to squeeze out some of the moisture from the long coat whilst the dog is still standing in the bath and then wrap him up in a large, warm towel and lift him out. Again, do not use a rubbing motion with the towel but rather 'pat' out any excess moisture. You may wish to use a second towel when the first one has absorbed most of the water and then lie him down, as described earlier, on your grooming table.

Using a specially designed dog hairdryer has two main advantages. It is more powerful and so dries the dog more quickly and, because it is mounted on a stand, both your hands are left free to groom your dog. As a result use of a canine dryer will speed up the process quite considerably. A good dryer, though involving a substantial initial outlay, will save you time and will give you many years' service, so it is worth considering.

However, if you wish to use an ordinary human-type dryer, and if there is a handyman around, it may well be possible to create some kind of device on which to balance the dryer so that you can still have both hands free. Naturally, any stand so designed must be completely safe and with no obstruction to any necessary air-flow. You must also be sure that the dryer will not over-heat; canine ones usually have three settings: hot, warm and cool. Another word of warning: take care that no part of the dryer, of whatever type, gets clogged with hair causing it to malfunction.

When drying your dog you will need to follow the same procedure as described earlier for general grooming. Never have the dryer too near to the coat or too hot. Many dogs object to a greater or lesser extent when air is blown on their heads, so leave the head until last so that it has already dried slightly in the general warmth of the surrounding air. Take care never to blow directly on to the head, and protect the eyes with your free hand.

Modhish Jack Flash. A full-coated youngster groomed for the show ring.

Your dog should always be dried immediately after a bath; never leave him for a while to dry off naturally for, apart from the fact that the dog could get cold, the coat will probably not dry completely straight but may tend to curl or even frizz.

The appearance of your freshly bathed Apso will be well worth the effort you have put in. Somehow they seem to know they look good. 'Just look at me', he will say to you. And, when the job is complete, always remember to praise him for having been so patient. You will both need patience at first but the rewards will be great.

Toe Nails

As mentioned earlier, the frequency with which your dog's nails will need clipping will depend very much upon the types of surface it lives and moves on. A dog kept in a carpeted house and exercised only on grass will need its nails clipped far more regularly than one which has a concrete kennel run, for example.

Clipping nails is not difficult, provided that you have taught your Apso to be well behaved and that you take care not to cut into the blood vessels which run through the nails. Pale-coloured nails are easier to trim than dark ones for you can see the blood vessels quite clearly through the former, whilst it is very much a matter of guesswork with the latter. It is wise, therefore, to clip just a little of the nail at a time. If there is any sign of blood or moisture stop immediately, and squeeze the end of the nail to stem any flow. You should, of course, try to avoid contact with the blood vessels and indeed your dog will probably 'tell' you when you are getting too near. It is worth keeping some potassium permanganate in the medicine cupboard to stop the bleeding in case of accident.

Keeping nails in trim is a very important aspect of canine grooming for if left to get too long the feet will splay out and the nail will be pressed into the foot as the dog walks. In extreme cases of neglect the nails curl right around and into the pad. Do not forget, either, that your dog may have dew claws (not only on the forelegs but sometimes on the hind ones too). These nails will certainly need clipping for they do not come into contact with the ground and will therefore not wear down naturally.

Teeth

You should always keep a check on your Apso's teeth and see to it that any tartar which may have formed is removed. There are some dog toothpastes available or, alternatively, it is possible to scale the teeth yourself, but I would not recommend that you do this unless you have had expert tuition. It is of course possible for your vet to scale the teeth fully but, in any event, you can help to keep the teeth relatively free from tartar by providing occasional hard biscuits to chew on; cows' hooves, now obtainable from many pet shops, can also be useful in this respect.

Anal Glands

I have left this until last for not everyone will either wish to or have the confidence to clear the anal glands and if you feel at all reticent about it, leave it to your vet. There are two trains of thought on this subject: indeed it is true that, once cleared, the glands will regularly need attention. I have dogs whose glands I have never needed to empty but if a dog shows any sign of discomfort around the back end then I feel his glands should be checked and, if necessary, emptied.

In the Apso the glands can be felt as two hazelnut-sized lumps, situated just below the surface, one on either side of the anal opening. Before bathing, or in the bath if you wish, apply gentle pressure to the glands with your thumb and forefinger to expel an unpleasant brown matter via the anus. Be sure to have tissues at the ready for this can be a rather messy business if the glands are full.

Naturally, if you prefer not to do this yourself it is a very simple matter for the vet to carry out when your dog goes for one of its routine visits, such as for a booster jab.

Wrapping the Coat

Very few exhibitors in the UK actually wrap the coat and I have no desire to describe how this is done since it is something I have never practised personally. I mention it purely to avoid confusion if a reader hears of 'wrapping' from some other source.

Wrapping is, briefly, dividing the coat into several sections and enclosing each section in a wrapper to protect the ends. It is time-consuming and takes practice. Readers will be relieved to know that the vast majority of the splendidly coated Lhasa Apsos to be seen in the UK show rings today have never had a 'wrapper' anywhere near them!

If You Prefer To Keep Your Apso Clipped Down

If you need or choose to keep your Apso in short coat, unless you are experienced with a pair of clippers you will probably wish to have this done by a professional at a grooming parlour. You are likely to need to take him for a clip every three to six months. An Apso which has been clipped does, however, still need to be groomed regularly although this, of course, will take much less time if the dog has a short coat. A coat which has been clipped will usually tend to grow in somewhat thicker than one which has not.

There are a number of 'styles' from which to choose, depending largely upon personal taste. You may prefer your Apso to be short all over which makes the coat ultra-easy to care for, or it could be short on the body and legs but with the head furnishings and tail left long. It is also possible simply to leave the tail long.

Should you decide to clip your Apso yourself don't rush into buying a pair of clippers (which are expensive) unless you are sure you know how to use them successfully. It is possible to clip down with scissors but you must be so very careful not to cut into the skin – especially vulnerable are ears and nipples.

Think, too, about the shock to the system if a dog is to suddenly undergo a transformation from long to short coat. Avoid, if possible, taking such a drastic measure just as winter is setting in. If, for some reason, you do have to clip down as the season is changing or in cold weather make sure the dog has extra bedding to keep him warm.

Daily Up keep

- If your Apso is allowed to run free in the garden, or if he goes on walks which enable him to pick up pieces of debris from the ground, make sure any foreign objects are removed without delay. Any little bits and pieces left in the coat will work their way into the undercoat where they will rapidly form knots and tangles.
- If your Apso gets a little wet after exercise keep a towel handy to dry him off as soon as he comes into the house or goes back in his kennel. And remember – don't rub.
- It is always worth keeping a can of flea spray (preferably obtained from your vet) in the cupboard, just in case a stray flea is noticed. If you use an insecticidal shampoo you will already have waged part of the war against these unpleasant intruders, but you can never be too sure.

  Do not, however, spray unless you believe it to be necessary and always take care not to spray into the mouth, eyes or nose. Be sure, too, that there is no food (for either canine or human consumption) in the vicinity. Follow the instructions on the can and never spray young puppies.

● You can consider yourself very lucky if you never have dirty bottom to contend with occasionally. This usually occurs if the motions are rather loose, perhaps due to a change of diet or even a change in temperature. Keep an eye out for the problem so that it can be dealt with immediately it arises. Your Apso will be grateful for your assistance and will usually sit quietly on the edge of the bathroom sink, clasped in the crook of your left arm whilst you rinse away with the right. You can, of course, carry out this rather unpleasant operation in the bath if you prefer but in this way one tends to get wet legs and feet unnecessarily.

7   Show Training and Shows

Hopefully when you purchased your puppy you made it clear to the breeder that you did or did not want to show. Even so, if you were sold a puppy with 'show potential' there is absolutely no guarantee (in *any* breed) that your puppy will turn out to be a top prize winner. The older the puppy is when it leaves the breeder, though, the more chance he or she will have of knowing its potential. Sometimes a breeder will 'run a puppy on' for show, keeping it until the age of about five or six months to see more clearly how it is developing; if it does not come up to scratch it will be sold as a pet and you will just have to be patient.

So much can change in an Apso puppy. The teeth may not come through as they should – even though it is usually possible to see if the jaw is broad enough, too few teeth may develop and a full set of first teeth does not necessarily mean that the second set will be complete. The upper jaw may grow too much in comparison with the lower one, giving the adult dog a scissor bite or an overshot mouth. If the lower jaw grows too much the adult will be too undershot. In the male there is a chance that perhaps only one testicle may descend. The bones of the legs develop slowly and may not end up quite as the breeder would have wished, or the dog may end up a little too long in the back, or too short in the back for that matter. I say again, so much can change.

But if the breeder truly knows her own stock and has used a stud dog with whose breeding she is familiar, she will have a fair idea of how the puppy is likely to progress, so if you have chosen your breeder with care you should allow yourself to be guided by her.

All, however, does not depend on the puppy itself; a lot depends upon you. If you are to stand any chance of substantial success in this competitive breed you must learn *how* to show. You must know how to present your Apso to his best advantage so that he looks just as good as he possibly can, whether stacked (standing) or on the move.

You will have begun to practise almost as soon as the puppy comes into your possession; as the dog grows older continue to practise for short spells each time. The front feet should be placed squarely under the dog's front assembly, the legs as straight as possible and the feet pointing forward. By the way, never use force of any kind – if the dog's forehand is not all you would wish for you'll just have to make the best of it! Also keep in mind that as a puppy's bones grow the rather knobbly bits you can feel usually straighten out, at least to some extent (!), as the leg height increases.

The back legs should not be placed too close together but nor should they be stretched widely apart. As you place your hand discreetly under the chin to lift the head so that it points straight forward, you should be able to see that the dog's topline is virtually straight, with just a gentle curve down from the withers, but on no account should there be any roach or dip. Neither should the back end rise in the adult, but you do frequently see a young puppy a little high on the back end. This will usually drop into place as the dog develops more height in its forequarters.

Place the tail over the back (unless it immediately goes there of its own accord!) so that the tip of the tail falls on the show side to give a more complete overall picture to the judge. If you wish you can comb the tail furnishings so that they fall on both sides of the body but you will only be able to do this successfully if the dog has a heavily furnished tail, which will come with maturity. Train your Apso to stay in this position whilst you touch up the ends of his coat with your brush or comb.

You will need to train your dog to stand in this manner on a table and on the ground, for he will have to do both when show time finally comes around. To get a good picture of him as the judge will see him

Ch Keiwa Mr Htut of Belazieth. Sire: Ch Belazieth's Salt 'n' Pepper. Dam: Larkwood Anthea. Bred by Mr and Mrs J. Bennett, during his show career Htut was owned by Mr and Mrs R. G. Richardson. He won 17 Challenge Certificates in a period of 15 months, his title having been won with Best of Breed at Cruft's in 1986.

you can practise in a mirror or get someone else to look on and tell you whether you have him stacked to best advantage. If you have friends whom you can trust to be gentle and sensible with the dog, ask them to 'go over' him on the table so that he will become accustomed to what will happen to him on the judging table.

Your dog must learn to know the difference between going for a romp in the park and moving round the show ring. Again ask someone else to watch as you move him so that you can learn to use the pace which is right for your dog. Move too quickly or too slowly and the dog will probably do strange things with his legs, and faults in construction are exaggerated on the move. Every dog has his own best pace; it is up to you to find it, and, when you have done so, teach the dog to use it automatically in the ring without your having to string him up on a tight lead for, if you do this, you will not allow his movement to be free.

Unless you live in a particularly out-of-the-way part of the country you will very probably find that a ringcraft class is held, perhaps one evening each week, relatively near to your home. This, as opposed to an obedience class, is specifically for the purpose of training dogs for the show ring. Do bear in mind, though, that those who run such classes usually do so purely for pleasure and, although most of them know their own breed, they may know nothing at all about Apsos. Nor will they necessarily be judges themselves, so do take extreme care in assessing whether those going over the dogs at a ringcraft class are doing so in what you consider to be a careful manner. Attending a ringcraft class can be an excellent way of training your young puppy (provided, of course, that it has completed its vaccination programme) but the wrong person going over your Apso can do more harm than good, so do take care. The Kennel Club can provide a list of registered ringcraft clubs but if you know of anyone locally who is a keen and, better still, successful exhibitor of Lhasa Apsos or one of the other smaller breeds, ask his or her advice as to which ringcraft class would be best for you. The cost of attending such a class is very small, usually there is a token annual subscription and then one pays a small amount each time one visits, the object, usually, being just to cover the cost of hiring the hall.

When your puppy is six months old he will be eligible to be exhibited in shows, providing that he is on the Kennel Club's Active Register and registered in your name. If you have sent off the appropriate forms to the Kennel Club but are still awaiting their return, you need to add NAF (name applied for) and/or TAF (transfer applied for) after the name of the dog when you fill in your show entry form. Bearing in mind that entry forms usually have to be submitted anything between three and eight weeks before the show date, you should start to look out for suitable shows well in advance. There are many types of show and space available in a breed book does not allow me to delve too deeply into these, so we shall concern ourselves here primarily with Championship and Open shows, for these are the two types in which you are most likely to find Lhasa Apso classes scheduled. At neither type of show are you obliged to become a member of the society holding the show if you exhibit, but in many cases you may do so if you wish. If you are fortunate enough to win a trophy, sometimes the trophy may not be collected by the winner unless he or she is a member.

Showing is an expensive hobby and prize money is rare these days, so even if you are fortunate enough to win a first prize do not necessarily expect to recover your entry fee, certainly not at a Championship show where entry fees are substantially higher than at other types of show.

If dog shows are new to you, you would be well advised to go along to watch a few before you take a dog along for exhibition. In this way you can observe ring procedure and pick up one or two tips from the ringside so that you will, when the great day comes (and I think all of us remember our very first show), be better prepared. For example, if your dog is a little on the large side do not stand him next to the smallest exhibit in the class (and vice versa); if your dog is a little short in coat you will want to avoid being next to one in full bloom. And if you know that Mrs So-and-So is an awful chatterbox do not stand next to her – you will want to concentrate one hundred per cent on your dog and will have no time for long, involved conversations with your neighbour. Watch, too, how exhibitors move to the table to set up their dogs whilst the previous exhibit is being moved. Doing this will give you as much time as possible to set up your dog so that he looks his best when the judge turns to look at him, but never, under any circumstances, obstruct the judge's view of the preceding dog.

When the time comes for the judge to pull out the award winners you will notice how the experts keep one eye on their dog and the other on the judge. In doing so they will not miss the opportunity of being granted further consideration if the judge wishes them to move their dog again, or if he brings them into the centre of the ring with a handful of others to be considered for the final class placings. Even when the judge appears to have placed the dogs in the order of his choice you will notice that the seasoned exhibitor still keeps showing because it is not unusual for the judge to alter some of the placings, seemingly at the very last minute.

Something else you will have to do before finally taking your puppy proudly to a show is to be sure you have the equipment you will need. All general Championship shows are benched, that it to say, each exhibit is allocated a small area, raised from the ground, and enclosed on three sides, either by wood or by metal. Strictly speaking, unless it is being groomed, exercised or exhibited, your dog is to spend the remainder of the day on its bench so you will almost certainly need a crate in which it will feel safe and secure. Just occasionally some exhibitors use a benching chain to attach their dog to the bench but unless you are going to keep constant vigil by your dog I do not recommend this for a dog as small as an Apso.

The best place at which to find a good selection of crates is at a Championship dog show. They come in a variety of sizes so choose that which you feel will be most convenient for you, bearing in mind that the dog must have ample room in which to stand up fully and to turn around. If, however, you choose a crate which is particularly large you will find that it may not fit on your bench, for benches are not always as wide as one would like.

You may, at first, not like the idea of your darling little Apso being subjected to such surroundings but he will soon get to like the idea and most dogs (I, personally, have one exception!) will look upon their crate as their home from home on show day. Inside the crate you will need a piece of bedding such as 'Vetbed' or something similar and it is also possible to buy a plastic or nylon cover for the crate to protect the dog from rain.

Your crate will, if you have chosen wisely, be of the variety that folds up so it is conceivably possible to walk from car to bench with dog, crate and grooming equipment, always assuming that you can find a suitable surface on which to groom. However, car parks are rarely as close to the benching areas as one would like, so if you have also brought a picnic, flask of coffee, extra woolly jumper and perhaps a portable table upon which to groom, you will find yourself quite out of puff upon your arrival! You may also have had to walk what seems like miles up and down the benches to locate your number, for they rarely seem to run in sequence and, if they do, you almost invariably enter the tent at the wrong end.

When you have struggled along in this fashion for a couple of shows you will come to realise that a trolley table or trolley is also a very worthwhile investment if you are a Lhasa Apso exhibitor! The trolley table was briefly described earlier; it folds down and can be pulled along with all your goods and chattels on the top and it can, of course, also be used as a grooming table both at home and at the show.

The alternative is a straightforward trolley, usually a little lighter in weight and easier to pull, but slightly less versatile. If I am taking only one or two dogs to a show I usually take a trolley with a crate on top and a good thick rubber car mat on top of the trolley to act as a surface

on which to groom. I find it almost as good as the table and far less cumbersome. Perhaps one of the funniest sights to newer exhibitors is witnessing the arrival of two or three people who have travelled together with maybe a dozen dogs between them, all of which are piled high in their crates on top of one trolley. It really is a work of art – or perhaps a feat of engineering, I am honestly not sure which!

Memories of Yesteryear. This charming photo shows the Lhasa Apsos Satroma, Sona and Satru. If you look closely you will see that ladies kept their handbags in their crates even then!

You will already have begun to see that showing is not going to be a cheap affair. If you are going to show seriously you will have to travel up and down the country, possibly every other weekend on average between spring and autumn, albeit less frequently in the winter months. There are not only the general Championship shows to attend but also the Championship show run by the British Utility Breeds Association and the various breed club shows at Open and Championship level. Campaigning a dog seriously takes time, money and commitment.

Not only is there the cost of petrol and sometimes parking, the entry fee per dog can presently be anything up to £10 for one class and you will most probably want to buy a catalogue so that you can follow the judging, knowing which dog is which in the various classes. Then you have to eat (a picnic is a good idea if you have had time to prepare it after you have bathed your dog) and there is always the temptation to down umpteen cups of coffee or the odd ice-cream.

But you do not have to begin with Championship shows – indeed it is a very good idea to begin by entering Open shows where the competition is less fierce, entry fees are lower and the car park is usually nearer to your destination. Because there is no benching you can manage without a crate if you are prepared to walk or carry your dog around with you all the while, so your initial outlay need not be so great. See how you enjoy a few Open shows before you start on the Championship circuit. It will be good practice for you and your dog and often the atmosphere is a little less intense. You will also probably have much more chance of being 'in the cards' for there are, except at breed club Open shows, usually fewer dogs in each class. On the negative side, you will not have the opportunity to see so many Apsos as you will at a Championship show for there will not be so many classes scheduled for the breed.

Not all Open shows offer classes for Apsos so you will, of course, have to check this at the time of making your entry. To find out about forthcoming shows you will need to purchase either (or both) of the two weekly canine newspapers, *Dog World* and *Our Dogs*. They may be available at some of the larger newsagents but it is safer to order your copies for newsagents rarely seem to carry a large stock.

Before you take your dog in the ring do be sure that he has had ample opportunity to relieve himself and you will, naturally, have checked that his coat is in tip-top condition. Many dogs seem reluctant to drink at shows but, especially if it is a hot day, see to it that your dog has been offered water shortly before his class for, in a big entry, he could be standing in the heat for quite a while. In any event, he will probably welcome a drink when he comes out of the ring so don't overlook this simple but important point in your excitement – he deserves it whether he has won or lost.

Check, in good time, whether your ring number is to be found on the bench, at the secretary's table (at Open shows) or whether it will be given to you in the ring. You want to avoid any last-minute panic and, in case you don't already have one (or have left a dozen at home!), you will be able to buy a ring-clip for a few pence at most shows.

It is good to win but it is also quite an achievement to be second, so if you have been awarded the blue card (we all know that in your heart of hearts you would really have liked the red one!) it is common practice to congratulate the lucky winner. There is no need to go overboard with your praise; a quick 'Well done' is enough. One day it may be you standing at the front of the line and you will appreciate that word of congratulation from behind. If you lose, do so graciously, there is always another judge and another day and if your dog is good enough, presented well and if you have the interest to persevere, your day will come.

If or when you do meet with success, be sure to keep track of your placings. Indeed, even if you have not been placed it is wise to keep a record of the judges under whom you have entered. If, in your opinion, your dog looked his best, performed well and the judge still 'threw him out' (did not place him) you will not wish to travel 200 miles with the same dog to be scrutinised by the same judge next year!

A very accurate record must be kept of all first prize awards for, other than in classes restricted simply by age, it is the number of wins in classes at certain levels which determines whether or not your dog is eligible for entry in a particular class. You will find the Kennel Club rulings about this inside each schedule, so check them carefully against your record of wins each time you enter. If your dog does a great deal of winning in the breed as a youngster you will also need to keep a careful record of the number of points he has scored towards his Junior Warrant. One point is gained for a first prize awarded at an Open show and three points for a first prize at a Championship show where Challenge Certificates are on offer for the breed. If twenty-five points are gained by the time he is eighteen months you will be able to apply to the Kennel Club for the Warrant, but this will entail completing a form asking precise details of when, where and in which classes the first prizes were awarded. And remember, this applies *only* to wins in classes for Lhasa Apsos; an Any Variety Tibetan class, for example, does not count.

Other special awards are Challenge Certificates (CCs) and Reserve Challenge Certificates (Res. CCs), Best Puppy and Best of Breed. Sometimes there are also awards for Reserve Best of Breed or Best Opposite Sex. At breed club shows there are an infinite number of special awards and at club shows someone with a successful exhibit can go home with an armful of trophies. These will generally have been donated by members of the club and are to be competed for annually.

Without doubt the Challenge Certificate is the most important award. At Championship shows the judge may award one each to the best dog and to the best bitch, and a dog is awarded the title of Champion if it has won three Challenge Certificates under three separate judges. One Challenge Certificate must have been given after the age of twelve months but in Apsos it would be highly unusual for this technicality to come into operation as usually only mature dogs in full coat achieve such honours – remember, too, that the judge can withhold the Challenge Certificate if he thinks fit. It sounds simple, doesn't it? But competition is strong in the breed and to make up a champion

Three winning dogs at Richmond Championship Show, 1938.

invariably takes a great deal of dedication and effort on the part of the exhibitor, not to mention all the attributes required in the dog, who in all probability has to beat other dogs who are already champions in order to get his 'tickets'.

Just one small point, but one which could save the newcomer some embarrassment. Just as a dog which is new to the ring (and has therefore never been awarded a first prize) is eligible to enter the Open class so, too, is a top winner or even a champion, even though the latter may be ineligible to enter the lower classes. You will see then that competition in the Open class is (usually) the strongest of all, so do not be misled by the description at the back of the schedule which states 'For all dogs ... etc.' There must be nothing more embarrassing for a newcomer to enter 'Novice' and 'Open' or, worse still, every class listed. This little piece of advice may sound banal but, believe me, I've seen it done more times than you can imagine!

Well, if you've read this chapter and still want to have a go at showing you will very probably join the rest of us who have been bitten by the show bug. You will go to bed exhausted in the small hours after preparing your dog, you will rise at the crack of dawn and drive an interminable distance to the venue, you may or may not agree with the judge's placings and your bank balance will undoubtedly suffer as a result of your frequent escapades. But if you really have been bitten you will enjoy (almost) every minute and you, too, will be considered by your non-doggy friends and relatives to be as foolish as the author! Frankly, only *you* and other dog show exhibitors will have any real idea why you obtain so much enjoyment from the sport!

Three champions of the 1980s. All owned by Mrs R. Wallis, these three grey and white particolour champions are (from the left) Ch Follow That Dream of Viento, English & International Nordic Ch Right on Cue From Viento and Ch Viento Impossible Dream who actually gained her title in 1979.

Ch Brackenbury Tongi-Gyemo and Ch Cotsvale Meeru. Tongi-Gyemo, bred and owned by Miss Harding became a Champion in 1967. Meeru, bred and owned by Miss Wild, was made up in 1970.

Ch Nedlik Tender Touch and Ch Nedlik An-An. Both bred and owned by Mrs S. Ellis, Tender Touch gained her title in 1983, with Best of Breed at Cruft's that same year. An-An gained his title in 1984.

Spot Checks On Show Entries

Cruft's 1932 – 10 entries (under the name of Lhassa terriers).
Kennel Club Show 1934 – 13 Apsos making 19 entries.
Cruft's Golden Jubilee Show 1936 – 11 Apsos making 20 entries.
Brighton Show 1937 – 9 Apsos making 14 entries – 'a good muster'.
Kennel Club Show 1938 – 16 Apsos making 26 entries.
Richmond Championship Show 1949 – 9 Apsos making 19 entries.
Cruft's 1951 – 5 Apsos making 7 entries.
Cruft's 1953 – 5 Apsos.
Ladies' Kennel Association 1953 – 8 Apsos in two classes.
Ladies' Kennel Association 1957 – 15 entries in three classes.
Ladies' Kennel Association (Club Show) 1966 – 37 Apsos making 76 entries (new UK breed record).
West of England Ladies' Kennel Association 1968 – 56 dogs making 105 entries (new UK breed record).
Cruft's 1969 – 41 dogs.
Lhasa Apso Club Open Show 1969 (the first breed club Open show) – 91 Apsos, i.e. 44 dogs and 47 bitches (another record entry).
Cruft's 1971 – 44 dogs making 72 entries.
Cruft's 1972 – 32 dogs making 51 entries.
Cruft's 1976 – 'An entry of 67 of which 55 came before me.'
Cruft's 1981 – 94 Apsos making 117 entries.
British Utility Breeds Association 1985 – 215 Apsos making 248 entries.
Cruft's 1988 – 160 Apsos making 178 entries.

8   Breeding the Lhasa Apso

Whether Or Not To Breed?

Let us begin by thinking very seriously about the ethics of breeding. If you mate a bitch you must know that you will be available to spend as much time as necessary with her. You are bringing into this world puppies which you will have to look after for *at least* eight weeks and you should, as a responsible breeder, be prepared to deal with any questions or worries that the new owners may encounter during the coming months. This support should be available throughout the puppy's life should it be required. If a puppy which you have sold for some reason needs to be re-homed it is your moral duty as a breeder to help in this situation and, if possible, take the unfortunate dog into your home or kennel until a new and suitable home has been found. It is an enormous responsibility.

If you feel that you want to breed to make a little spare cash then stop reading now, for that is certainly *not* what breeding is all about! Indeed there are few dedicated breeders who make any substantial profit out of their puppies when all their expenses have been taken into consideration. Those who do make a profit probably breed as part of a larger canine enterprise which involves showing, boarding and possibly grooming dogs, as well as breeding them.

You will need a not inconsiderable amount of capital to breed your first litter and you cannot cut down on necessities with the intention of buying them for the next litter 'if this one turns out all right'. By cutting corners and having too little spare cash available for vets' bills, which almost inevitably arise, you risk the health and possibly the lives of both puppies and bitch. Your bitch and her puppies will be dependent entirely upon you for their needs and you must see to it that you have the time, knowledge, resources and finance to provide that support.

Let me say now that you cannot successfully hold down a full-time job and give the puppies the attention they deserve. You may, perhaps, be able to take a couple of weeks' 'vacation' around the time of the whelping but unless you have responsible and capable members of the family or a professional kennel-maid to look after them during the day-time (*every* day) you really should not contemplate bringing a litter into the world.

All this may sound very negative but I believe it is only fair to the dogs in question to be responsible and realistic about the whole affair before you begin. Breeding a litter sounds very appealing but it is not for the faint-hearted, or for the squeamish. Most Apsos give birth with relative ease compared with some of the brachycephalic (short-nosed) breeds, but they seem rarely to be self-whelpers, that is to say that you need to be on hand to help at the birth, particularly to break the sac and cut (or tear) the umbilical cord. Indeed I am sure that there are occasions when bitches have whelped successfully on their own but this should never be allowed to happen as the risk of distress and danger to the bitch and her puppies is great.

There have been several very good books written about whelping and weaning and if you are contemplating your first litter of puppies you should read up as much as you can well in advance so that you have inwardly digested the contents thoroughly before the day of the whelping arrives. Do not leave it until the last few days to get hold of the book you had promised yourself – your bitch may whelp early! And be sure that the book is near to hand in the whelping room for it is quite surprising how one's mind goes blank in a time of crisis and you cannot recall exactly what the book said you should do next when the problem occurs!

So, assuming that you have decided to breed a litter, and feel sure that your bitch is soundly constructed and of good enough 'breed type' to do so, let us now consider how you should best go about it and what equipment will be needed.

Age of Bitch

It is generally accepted that an Apso should not be allowed to have a litter until she is about eighteen months old, so if your bitch came into season at six months and again at twelve months, the second season will be too soon. If, however, her second season were to fall at the age of fifteen or sixteen months, that would probably be all right. In giving these guidelines I am not saying that a younger bitch would not be capable of producing puppies and raising a litter (she probably would), but she would not be mature enough, either mentally or physically, and, when breeding, your first duty must always be to your bitch.

I hesitate to give guidelines as to the maximum age at which a bitch can successfully produce a litter – some seem to be able to go on for ever – but I would exercise great caution over the age of seven. I feel that an Apso's first litter should, ideally, be produced by the time she is about four. There are always exceptions and so very much depends upon the bitch herself, so if you have any doubts as to her suitability from the point of view of physical condition or age then you would be wise to seek a vet's advice.

Choice of Stud

For your first litter it is often sensible to seek the advice of your bitch's breeder as to which stud dogs she would consider suitable for the bitch. Very serious thought must be given to the choice of stud and there is nothing more heart-breaking for a breeder than to find that someone to whom you have sold a puppy bitch has eventually mated her to a dog that in your opinion is totally unsuitable; although, naturally, the owner of the bitch is at liberty to use whichever dog she will, unless a special breeding agreement has been entered into. Often pet owners have no conception of the hours of planning and years of careful breeding that went into producing the litter from which they selected their pup. In consequence, almost without thinking, they may use the 'Apso which lives round the corner' or even a top winning dog which

Jonters Benito. Sire: Fr Imp Saluq Annapurna Quapito. Dam: Torrens Eva. A great favourite of Mr J. Ford, his breeder and owner, Ben was also much loved by Mrs Di Trudgill to whom this book is dedicated.

they happen to like but which does not, in any way, complement the bitch in question.

Two factors come into play: the phenotype and the genotype. Very briefly, breeding for phenotype involves selection on the basis of appearance and traits which are expressed in the dog, whereas genotype involves selecting on the basis of the dog's genetic make-up, even though the dog himself may not necessarily express the traits he carries. Frequently a combination of the two is used in selecting the dog of your choice.

It would be possible to write for hours on this very subject but unfortunately space does not permit. Some of the information contained in Chapter 11 may, however, be of special interest and I have included some worthwhile reading material in the bibliography.

You cannot be too careful in selecting your sire and you should try to select for features which you feel will enhance your bitch's weaker points. In its simplest form, if your aim, for example, is to improve coat texture then your ideal will probably be to select a dog with good coat texture himself and known to throw good coat texture in his offspring. Naturally, you cannot, however, select a sire on the strength of this one good feature but you will have to weigh up all his strengths and weaknesses against the virtues or otherwise of your own bitch. You will therefore have to look very carefully not only at the stud dogs available but also at what they have produced. Remember, too, that they have not only produced the dogs and bitches you see in the ring but undoubtedly many more which have been sold as pets. You will see, therefore, that you are about to embark on a rather difficult task, one in which it is only too easy to make mistakes.

If it is your bitch's first litter it is wise to use a dog which is a proven sire for he will be experienced and will usually (but not always) treat the bitch with consideration and show her what to do (if she *needs* showing!). Added to this, if you use a maiden dog you will not have had the opportunity to have seen his offspring, nor will you be sure that he is actually potent. If for some reason (and sometimes there really *are* good reasons) you do wish to mate your maiden bitch to a maiden dog you would be wise to have a 'back-up' in case you do not manage to obtain a mating; possibly the dog's sire would be a suitable choice if he is available.

Whatever your choice of sire, you will be doing one of three things – inbreeding, linebreeding or outcrossing. Again I must suggest that you read more comprehensive books on this subject and would refer you to the last chapter of this book for further reference. However, I would definitely not recommend a novice breeder to inbreed or to linebreed too closely (and there are varying views as to where inbreeding ends and linebreeding begins), for, in doing so, you will bring out both faults and virtues in your puppies and you must know how to deal with problems if they arise.

When you are clear in your own mind as to which stud dog you would like to use ask the owner of that dog, as soon as possible, whether you may indeed use his services on your bitch and, if so, establish the fee to be paid. Some dogs are at 'public stud' but others are at 'limited stud to approved bitches only', so it is possible that if the owner of a stud dog does not consider your bitch a suitable 'partner' your request will be refused. I have an unpleasant feeling that the latter is rapidly becoming a thing of the past which is sad, because if more stud dog owners refused poor-quality bitches the stock in this country today would undoubtedly be more consistent both in type and in quality. But here is not the place to pursue that train of thought!

Do be sure to advise the owner of the dog just as soon as your bitch comes into season and be sure to check her every day so that there can be no mistake as to which actually is her first day.

The Time for Mating

Your bitch will be ready for mating only for a short spell during her season. There is absolutely no hard-and-fast rule as to which days of the season are the ones on which she is 'right'. One does get to know one's own bitches, and how early or late a bitch is ready seems to vary from line to line. Most of my own bitches are ready between the tenth and thirteenth days but I have had others ready as early as the seventh day. Having said that, several visiting bitches have not been ready until the sixteenth day or later, and I have heard of some mated as late as the twenty-third, so virtually anything is possible. Mid-season is, however, perhaps the most usual in Apsos and often the bitch will only accept a dog for two, three, or perhaps four days. There are, of course, exceptions and you will need to check the bitch's vulva regularly, for if you follow normal practice you will give dog and bitch one day of rest between the first and second matings. A second mating is not essential but is usually advisable, especially in the case of a dog which is not used at stud on a very regular basis for some of the semen can become stale.

As the bitch approaches her time of readiness her vulva will be enlarged and if you place your thumb horizontally across the top you will find that it has softened. It would be wise to feel the vulva at the beginning of her season so that you can more easily compare. As she approaches readiness her tail will almost inevitably move to one side as you touch her back end, but many bitches will indeed move their tail in this way not only when they are ready for mating. By the time she is ready she will probably have stopped losing colour or the colour may have paled, but not necessarily so.

Where to Mate

In most cases it is common for the bitch to visit the dog, and in many cases stud dogs will perform better in their own familiar surroundings.

If you have chosen a stud dog which is some considerable distance from your home the dog's owner may be prepared to keep your bitch for a few days to save you a double trip, especially if on your first visit you do not achieve a mating. Be sure to check this with the owner of the stud dog at the time of enquiry for many of the smaller breeders simply do not have the space or facility to keep an extra bitch which is in full season, for her very presence may play havoc with any dogs in the vicinity. If you can leave your bitch for a few nights you must be prepared to pay a fee for her lodgings if requested, and make sure you take her own blanket and possibly also her own bed or crate if the stud dog owner requires it. Many owners are reluctant to be parted from their bitches so you may, of course, be quite prepared to travel daily. But, just to put your mind at rest, I find that most bitches settle down quite happily for their short stay, although one or two have been quite extraordinarily finicky about their food.

The Mating

If you are present for the mating do not take the entire family – this will almost certainly disturb the dog and very probably the bitch too, not to mention your host! The owners of the stud dog should know exactly how they would like to carry out the mating and it is unlikely that they will wish to have more than one extra person present in the room or mating area.

Even though your bitch may never have been mated before she will probably play up to the dog and, indeed, it is a delight to see a dog and bitch frolicking together for a few minutes or so before the actual mating. There are, unfortunately, other bitches who seem to sit there like stuffed dummies and do little to encourage the dog and these, especially, are the bitches who need to go to experienced studs, for they will do nothing to assist a young, inexperienced dog.

A mating usually involves two persons (as well as the dogs!): one to keep a firm grip under the chin of the bitch who, by the way, should be wearing a proper leather collar for there is always the possibility that she may snap, however good her temperament. She may also, if you are unlucky, make noises as if she is being tortured but these usually subside a moment or two after the dog has penetrated. The other person will see to the back end and support the bitch's back legs and abdomen whilst the dog mounts. Great care must be taken, however, not to obstruct the dog in any way. If the dog is having some difficulty in entering the bitch it may be due to a difference in size. In such circumstances a mating may be more easily effected by placing a folded blanket under either dog or bitch to compensate. Some breeders like to use a little KY jelly or Vaseline for lubrication purposes but I prefer not to unless the dog seems to be having particular difficulty.

Immediately the dog has penetrated, the 'tie' will take place. This happens because the dog's penis swells and the muscles in the bitch's vagina grip it so tightly that the pair, quite simply, cannot part until the muscles relax. Very soon after the tie has begun the dog will wish to turn; this he will probably do himself but he may need a little guided assistance from his owner, though he must never be forced. The dog and bitch may end up back to back or in an 'L' shape or, almost unbelievably, the dog may lie down! The bitch often gets somewhat restless during the tie so you should remain with her so that she does not try to pull away from the dog to the discomfort of both and one must, of course, avoid anything which may cause injury to the dog who, when mating, is much more susceptible to injury than the bitch.

Perhaps the most usual length of time for a tie is something between seven and fifteen minutes but shorter ties (or in extreme cases no tie at all) can certainly result in puppies being born. Longer ties do also happen, twenty to thirty minutes is not infrequent, and I once recall missing the replay (I had not seen the match, nor had I heard the result) of the Wimbledon men's final when my dog tied for just over three-quarters of an hour. A tie lasting over an hour is not unknown! Do be sure that fresh drinking water is available at arm's length, for the dog, especially, may be grateful for a drink, however short the tie. Two of my own dogs always seem to bite their tongues at the moment of ejaculation, following which they immediately take a little drink, which seems to help.

When the time comes for dog and bitch to separate the stud will want to wash himself and check that his penis has returned to its sheath. You must of course follow the guidance of the stud dog owner but I, personally, like dog and bitch to have another ten minutes or so in each other's company, during which time they usually just wander about quietly or lie down together (they should not be allowed to frolic now). This gives them both a little time to unwind and gives their owners an opportunity to settle up the financial side of the affair. You must be sure that a very clear agreement is reached as to what procedure will be followed if the bitch fails to whelp. This is usually written on the receipt so that there can be no future misunderstanding. The stud fee you pay is for the service of the dog, not for the puppies which result, but most stud dog owners will provide a repeat mating at the bitch's next season if the bitch did not produce puppies the first time.

A Word About Care of the Stud Dog

A good stud dog is a very beneficial asset to a kennel and needs to be treated in rather a special way from the time he is a youngster, indeed as soon as the owner has decided that he is of good enough quality to be used at stud. Whilst still a youngster any sexual tendencies he may display must not be quelled. It is normal for there to be a certain amount of sex-play behaviour in a young male of about five or six months and often one tends to make an attempt to stop this, but a potential stud must not be reprimanded. If you feel that he is taking his sexual urge to extremes, which can happen, especially if he is with other youngsters, you would be advised to move him to the company of some older Apsos, a kindly middle-aged lady who has been spayed would perhaps be ideal. Naturally, unless you have a kennel of dogs you may not have any choice as to who the potential stud is to live with but he should be kept away from any bitch who is coming into season, just in case she snaps at him as a warning that she is not yet ready to mate. Such an incident could be very damaging to his potential stud career for he could be discouraged.

Many owners of Lhasa Apso stud dogs like a young stud to mate one or perhaps two bitches just before he is one year old, then he can be rested for a few months until he is more mature. Some owners allow him to be used as young as the age of eight months but I am one of many who would prefer him to be ten or eleven months. Certainly he must not be over-used at this early age but it does indeed seem that he has a better chance of becoming accustomed to stud work if first used whilst still relatively young. It is also to his advantage that if he is kept in a kennel he is brought into the house fairly frequently so that he feels comfortable in both sets of surroundings. Unfortunately stud dogs do have a habit of lifting their legs to mark territory, both indoors and outdoors. This is only to be expected and the dog should not be strongly scolded for his actions. Many owners have a special room set aside for matings to take place, rarely an appealing room according to human taste, but a personal little kingdom for the stud!

In ideal circumstances the young stud dog should first be mated to one of the owner's own bitches so that he can be proven, and the bitch should be one who is of sound temperament and who has had at least one previous litter so that she knows what she is doing. For the smaller kennel this is not always possible and here is one of the dilemmas inevitably encountered if one wishes to keep one or more stud dogs but does not wish to breed more than one or two litters a year. Before deciding to use a dog at stud, it is essential to bear in mind that he must be of good enough quality for his services to be in demand by owners of other bitches too, and one must never lose sight of the fact that there will undoubtedly be quite a substantial number of champions and top winning dogs available at stud throughout the beginnings of his own stud career. Another thing to be remembered is that an active stud dog should always be fed a carefully balanced, high-quality diet.

Something to Bear in Mind

If your bitch is mated, accidentally, to two dogs during the same season it is *possible* that she will 'take' to both sires. Of the puppies which therefore result, some will have one sire and some another. No puppy will have two sires (as is sometimes supposed!). Do therefore be extra careful if you are mating your bitch that no other male has access to her throughout the *entire* period of her season.

Is She in Whelp?

I suppose I have been lucky in that I have never mated one of my own bitches and later found that she did not produce puppies as a result. I suspect that Apsos 'miss' far less frequently than many other breeds. Indeed some bitches act as if they instinctively know that they are in whelp almost immediately after the mating. Quite often if the bitch has taken, her nipples seem to 'stand up' within the next few days following the mating and also her vulva does not shrink right down. It must be stressed, however, that none of these signs is any proof that she is definitely in whelp. Certainly you must not poke around in the abdomen to see 'if you can feel anything' – anxious as you are to know the outcome, just try to be patient. Growth of the puppies during the early weeks of pregnancy is very slow indeed, most of the growth in each foetus taking place during the final two weeks. Nevertheless, I usually have a fair idea as to whether or not the bitch is in whelp by the fourth to fifth week, although if you are not familiar with bitches in whelp you may have to wait a little longer before you can be sure.

The mammary glands usually start to develop more fully around the fifth week and by the seventh week they have started to become softer. Even before the puppies are born there is usually a fluid or actual milk present. In the fifth week the bitch may go off her food or seem to be a little more than usually fussy about it. She may, in some cases, perhaps also vomit slightly at about this time.

What Can I do to Help During Her Pregnancy?

By week six you should have a fairly good idea if she is in whelp. She will now need to eat about one-third more than her normal daily supply of food but you will need to feed her little and often (three or four small meals a day). She may at this time feel slightly 'off colour' and may, by choice, miss a meal or two.

Under no circumstances should you over-feed her from the time she is mated for you will only succeed in producing an overweight bitch and, in doing so, you will increase the possibility of her encountering whelping problems.

Neither should you give her a surfeit of supplements, but I do recommend proprietary multi-vitamin tablets as per the directions on the container. A calcium supplement will also be of help but opinions vary as to whether this should be given prior to whelping or immediately afterwards so it would be wise to consult your vet on this matter. Personally I give a liquid calcium supplement from the day of whelping.

She should continue to take regular exercise throughout her pregnancy but should not be allowed to over-exert herself and must have the opportunity to rest whenever she wishes. It is unwise for her to be in the company of any boisterous dogs from about the fourth week onwards and she should certainly be discouraged from jumping on the furniture.

Just a little word of caution here. It is perfectly possible for a bitch to begin to develop puppies, only later to reabsorb them at some stage during her pregnancy. The reasons for this peculiar and very unfortunate happening can be many and are frequently almost impossible to determine. If, after you have been sure that your bitch is carrying puppies, she then appears not to be in whelp, consult your vet immediately, for any undeveloped foetus not totally reabsorbed is likely to set up an infection. In any event you will wish to check that she is in good health and to discuss with your vet the possible reasons for the problem. Do bear in mind, however, that a bitch can often look quite heavily in whelp and then somewhat less so; this does not necessarily indicate that a problem is about to occur, merely that the puppies have moved position and are tucked up rather more under her ribcage. This can be especially obvious in the Lhasa Apso due to her overall body length and you will usually find that a shorter-coupled bitch looks rather more 'roly-poly' than one which is longer cast.

Prior to the whelping the bitch should not be over-fussed but she will need you there for reassurance, particularly if it is her first litter. You will also help her by seeing to it that everything you will need for the whelping is at hand. You may introduce her to the whelping box perhaps ten days or a week before she is due so that she gets used to it slowly and does not suddenly find herself sleeping in strange quarters the night before you expect her to whelp.

Her coat should have been kept well groomed throughout for she will not wish to be subjected to lengthy grooming sessions. About a week before she is due to whelp you can carefully cut the hair around her teats, although much of this will fall out of its own accord. You may find it wise also to trim a little around her back end so that she will stay as clean and dry as possible during the whelping. Some breeders, myself included, prefer to cut the bitch's coat short as soon as they know for certain that she is in whelp for, in doing so, not only does she feel nice and comfortable but the danger of her pups becoming entangled in the coat is reduced. Naturally, if you hope to put your bitch back into the show ring within the next year you will not be able to cut her coat to any great extent.

You can expect your bitch to whelp sixty-three days after the first mating but she could be a few days early or late so you must be completely prepared one full week before the due date. The whelping chart on page 118 will help you to plan:

Telephone your vet about one week before the due date so that he is forewarned should any unforeseen problems occur. Be sure that the vet's telephone number is immediately accessible at all times and remember that if you feel there is cause for concern a vet can be contacted at any time, twenty-four hours a day. Naturally, you should always try to be considerate and call at 'sociable hours' if possible, but if you get into difficulties do not risk the health of your bitch and her puppies by waiting until morning!

One last word before we move on to the great event: when in whelp (as at all times) make sure that when you pick up your bitch you support her not only at the front but also under her back end. You will find that if one hand goes under her bottom and grasps the outside leg, she will sort of perch comfortably on your hip, supported, of course, at the front end too. Avoid picking her up any more than necessary, especially during the last two or three weeks, and when you place her down be sure that she puts all four feet on the ground together and under no circumstances jumps out of your arms.

What You Will Need for the Whelping

WHELPING BOX Every breeder has a slight personal preference as to

Perpetual Whelping Chart

Mated Jan.	1 2 3 4 5	6	7	8	9 10 11 12 13 14 15 16 17 18 19 20 21 22 23 24 25 26 27		28 29 30 31
Due to whelp March	5 6 7 8 9	10	11	12 13 14 15 16 17 18 19 20 21 22 23 24 25 26 27 28 29 30 31	April	1 2 3 4

Mated Feb.	1 2 3 4 5	6	7	8	9 10 11 12 13 14 15 16 17 18 19 20 21 22 23 24 25 26		27 28
Due to whelp April	5 6 7 8 9	10	11	12 13 14 15 16 17 18 19 20 21 22 23 24 25 26 27 28 29 30	May	1 2

Mated Mar.	1 2 3 4 5	6	7	8	9 10 11 12 13 14 15 16 17 18 19 20 21 22 23 24 25 26 27 28 29		30 31
Due to whelp May	3 4 5 6 7	8	9 10 11 12 13 14 15 16 17 18 19 20 21 22 23 24 25 26 27 28 29 30 31	June	1 2

Mated Apr.	1 2 3 4 5	6	7	8	9 10 11 12 13 14 15 16 17 18 19 20 21 22 23 24 25 26 27 28		29 30
Due to whelp June	3 4 5 6 7	8	9 10 11 12 13 14 15 16 17 18 19 20 21 22 23 24 25 26 27 28 29 30	July	1 2

Mated May	1 2 3 4 5	6	7	8	9 10 11 12 13 14 15 16 17 18 19 20 21 22 23 24 25 26 27 28 29		30 31
Due to whelp July	3 4 5 6 7	8	9 10 11 12 13 14 15 16 17 18 19 20 21 22 23 24 25 26 27 28 29 30 31	August	1 2

Mated June	1 2 3 4 5	6	7	8	9 10 11 12 13 14 15 16 17 18 19 20 21 22 23 24 25 26 27 28 29		30
Due to whelp August	3 4 5 6 7	8	9 10 11 12 13 14 15 16 17 18 19 20 21 22 23 24 25 26 27 28 29 30 31	Sept.	1

Mated July	1 2 3 4 5	6	7	8	9 10 11 12 13 14 15 16 17 18 19 20 21 22 23 24 25 26 27 28 29		30 31
Due to whelp September	2 3 4 5 6	7	8	9 10 11 12 13 14 15 16 17 18 19 20 21 22 23 24 25 26 27 28 29 30	Oct.	1 2

Mated Aug.	1 2 3 4 5	6	7	8	9 10 11 12 13 14 15 16 17 18 19 20 21 22 23 24 25 26 27 28 29		30 31
Due to whelp October	3 4 5 6 7	8	9 10 11 12 13 14 15 16 17 18 19 20 21 22 23 24 25 26 27 28 29 30 31	Nov.	1 2

Mated Sept.	1 2 3 4 5	6	7	8	9 10 11 12 13 14 15 16 17 18 19 20 21 22 23 24 25 26 27 28		29 30
Due to whelp November	3 4 5 6 7	8	9 10 11 12 13 14 15 16 17 18 19 20 21 22 23 24 25 26 27 28 29 30	Dec.	1 2

Mated Oct.	1 2 3 4 5	6	7	8	9 10 11 12 13 14 15 16 17 18 19 20 21 22 23 24 25 26 27 28 29		30 31
Due to whelp December	3 4 5 6 7	8	9 10 11 12 13 14 15 16 17 18 19 20 21 22 23 24 25 26 27 28 29 30 31	Jan.	1 2

Mated Nov.	1 2 3 4 5	6	7	8	9 10 11 12 13 14 15 16 17 18 19 20 21 22 23 24 25 26 27 28 29		30
Due to whelp January	3 4 5 6 7	8	9 10 11 12 13 14 15 16 17 18 19 20 21 22 23 24 25 26 27 28 29 30 31	Feb.	1

Mated Dec.	1 2 3 4 5	6	7	8	9 10 11 12 13 14 15 16 17 18 19 20 21 22 23 24 25 26 27		28 29 30 31
Due to whelp February	2 3 4 5 6	7	8	9 10 11 12 13 14 15 16 17 18 19 20 21 22 23 24 25 26 27 28	March	1 2 3 4

the type of whelping box he or she prefers, but for an Apso it should be roughly 3 ft × 2 ft 6 ins (90 × 75 cm) or perhaps just a little larger. Again you will doubtless be reading more comprehensive books on the subject of whelping so you will be able to obtain a fair idea of how best such a box can be constructed. I do not, however, advocate that you can get by with large cardboard boxes as some authors suggest. You will need something more solid and it must be raised slightly from the ground to avoid draughts. Your whelping box should therefore be soundly constructed of new wood so that it will withstand a very thorough scrubbing down before it is stored away in readiness for the next litter. Meanwhile, it will have taken some tough treatment from a handful of very adventurous puppies!

Either the front panel should form a flap so that you can easily get at the bitch whilst she is whelping or, alternatively, it can have extra horizontal panels made to slot into the sides so that the height can be increased as the puppies grow. Your bitch must, however, be able to get in and out of the box at will so if the sides are higher to keep puppies in, do be sure that she has some facility for getting in and out as she wishes. As the box is raised a few inches from the floor it will be easier for her to get out than in so a little step placed on the outside of the box will usually suffice.

Most importantly, there should be a guard rail around the inside of the box. This should be about 3 ins (75 mm) from the floor of the box and should extend out by about 3 ins (75 mm) too. The guard rail should fit around all four sides and is to protect the puppies should they get trapped behind the bitch. I have only once whelped without a guard rail and that was the only occasion when the dam mistakenly 'sat' on a puppy. When such terrible accidents occur the puppy rarely has any chance to make a sound to let you know. In my own case I always sleep with the bitch and her whelps for the first nights to be sure that I am within earshot if needed. On that sad night I did not hear a thing.

The other item which I feel should be fitted is a heat lamp. This needs to be suspended above the box but you must have a facility for altering the height and it must, of course, be safe. It should be roughly 30 ins (75 cm) above the dam's back when she is standing, that is to say, approximately 40 ins (100 cm) from the base of the box.

Various types of heat lamp are available and may or may not give out light. For maximum protection it should be fitted with a protective 'cage'. I like to set it up slightly off-centre so that the bitch can keep clear of the direct heat if she wishes. If you choose a lamp which gives out heat only I strongly recommend that whilst the puppies are very small a dim light is left on in their room so that the bitch can see exactly what she is doing. Although the room temperature should, in any event, be kept warm, the puppies will benefit from heat, especially when the mother is away from the nest. Use of a heated pad which fits the bottom of the box is an alternative.

NEWSPAPER You will need an almost unbelievably plentiful supply of newspaper for the base of the whelping box for it will constantly need to be changed throughout the whelping process. If possible the newspaper should be unused so you should try to strike up a friendly relationship with your newsagent several weeks beforehand so that he will provide you with his unsold papers. Unfortunately such a supply is becoming more and more difficult to find as so many papers now have to be sent back for re-cycling. Nevertheless, do try, it will be well worthwhile if you can find a source.

KITCHEN TOWEL AND/OR TOWELS I like to have at least six rolls of *white* paper kitchen towel to hand, useful for so many things, including rubbing down the puppies. It is good to know that one is always using clean, dry pieces of towelling which can be thrown away immediately to save unnecessary clutter in the whelping process. Alternatively you may prefer to have a supply of clean white towels, or a combination of both. Proper babies' nappies are a very suitable size but by no means cheap – I gave up using such luxuries long ago! A towel will also be needed to wrap around your hot-water bottle (see below).

CLEAN WATER It is, of course, ideal if there is a washbasin in the whelping room but, if not, be sure to have a basin of water at the ready.

NAIL BRUSH AND SURGICAL SCRUB You (and your vet if he needs to visit) must be sure that your hands (and nails) are clean at all times.

TWO CARDBOARD BOXES One lined with 'Vetbed' or similar so that puppies can be put in here if necessary as each whelp arrives. The second, which must have a tight-fitting lid to it, is just in case you have dead or very badly malformed whelps. In such unfortunate circumstances these should be immediately removed from the whelping room so as not to upset the bitch any more than necessary.

HOT-WATER BOTTLE To be thoroughly wrapped in a towel and placed at the bottom of the first cardboard box, below the 'Vetbed'.

CLOCK, NOTEBOOK AND PENCIL You will want to keep an accurate record of timing between contractions and delivery of each whelp.

KITCHEN SCALES These should have as deep a tray as possible and will be used to weigh each puppy as soon as (or very soon after) it is born. A record should then be made of the puppies' weights for the next few weeks. I like to weigh *every* day for the first two weeks, then, if all appear to be making good progress, I weigh twice a week until they depart.

SCISSORS Sharp but blunt ended, preferably of the surgical variety.

STERILISING TABLETS Everything you need to use must be thoroughly sterilised.

MILD DISINFECTANT Disinfectant, used for whatever reason, must be mild and of the type which is suitable for cleansing wounds etc.

PLASTIC BAGS OR LIDDED BUCKETS For disposal of an ever-increasing mountain of soiled newspapers, kitchen towel and placentas. The whelping area should be kept tidy at all times.

PREMATURE BABY BOTTLE These are not always easy to obtain (try your local hospital if your vet, chemist or GP cannot assist) but a cat-feeding bottle can be used instead. Personally, however, I find that 'prem-baby' bottles are much easier to use. Be sure you have an ample supply of teats in stock – one is not enough.

MILK SUBSTITUTE A good quality proprietary milk substitute, designed specifically for puppies, may be needed if your bitch does not produce sufficient milk or if a puppy for some reason needs supplementary feeding by hand.

FLASK OF COFFEE AND PACKET OF BISCUITS These are for you, for once whelping starts you will have no time to see to yourself and whelping a bitch can take a good few hours! (Night-time whelpings always seem to make me hungry!)

9 Whelping and Weaning

Whelping Time

Let me begin by stressing that it is essential to read comprehensive books covering whelping in detail for, clearly, space here does not permit a thorough explanation.

Leading up to the time your bitch produces the puppies she will most probably have been 'nest making' and it is highly likely that she will go off her food for the last twenty-four hours or so. Her temperature will also have dropped at least one degree about twenty-four hours before the whelping begins.

When she goes out to spend a penny make sure she is clearly supervised (take a torch if necessary), for she may try to make her nest under a bush, which would be a most appropriate but highly inconvenient place to deposit her puppies! In addition you do not wish the first puppy to be born on your lawn without you knowing anything about it! Certainly she should not now come into contact with any other of your household pets and, worried though you may be, you should be in firm control for she will look to you for support.

As she gets closer and closer to producing the first puppy she will pant loudly which indicates nervous anticipation rather than pain. If all is running smoothly the vulva will by now be large, open and moist and you will see a fairly thick white discharge.

As she goes into the second stage of labour you should note down the time of her contractions, which will develop in frequency and strength until the first puppy is produced, usually within the hour. There is likely to be a sudden gush of fluid, a prelude to the puppy being forced out of the vagina, hopefully still in its sac. It is highly likely that the puppy will not be expelled entirely in one push but no puppy should be allowed to remain in the vaginal tract for too long because, with the passage of time, there is an increasing risk to the likelihood of survival. If a puppy does appear to have been born dead and you suspect, because of circumstances and the fact that it is otherwise 'perfectly' formed, that it died in the canal through lack of oxygen, take it in your two hands (one hand supports the head and the puppy should be face downwards) and swing it through the air, up and down, between your legs. In doing so you will get air into the lungs so that it will, hopefully, start breathing again and at the same time you will encourage the circulation of blood. It will not always work, of course, but I have used this method with success and have witnessed my vet do so too. Other breeders sometimes blow into the puppy's mouth but it is difficult in this way to ascertain how much air the puppy's lungs are capable of taking. If the tongue is white and the puppy seemingly more than recently dead you should not make an effort to revive it for prolonged lack of oxygen will have caused brain damage.

Many Apsos are born feet first, almost fifty per cent it seems. Provided that the puppy is facing downwards this is *not* a breech birth, although head-first puppies do seem to come a little more easily because the bulk of the head seems to stimulate the bitch rather more. A breech birth, which is feet first *and* upside down, is much more likely to cause difficulties because the shape of the puppy is not following the natural contours of the bitch as it passes through. There can be other forms of malpresentation which the experienced breeder may be able to correct, but in most cases veterinary assistance will be needed if there is any obstruction to the normal free passage of the puppy.

As soon as the puppy is safely out of the bitch you will need to break the sac if the bitch has not done so immediately. The bitch will not wish you to interfere more than necessary but if possible rub down the puppy with a towel and clear its mouth and nostrils of any fluid or mucus which remain. It is at this stage that I always check for cleft palate, for if I were unfortunate enough to find it I would rather do so sooner than later.

If the puppy has been produced head first but the bitch is taking a long time to expel the rest of the body, I like to break the sac and clear the air passages immediately. I have had many instances when the puppy has actually vigorously suckled the lower teats (for up to twenty minutes) whilst the body, back legs and placenta were still inside the bitch. Great care must be taken not to break the sac if the head of the puppy is still inside the bitch.

Should the bitch not break the umbilical cord herself (and in my experience Apsos rarely do) you will either need to tear it or cut it with *sterilised* scissors. I normally advocate tearing but I have had cords so tough that I have been quite unable to tear without risk of pulling too much on the puppy's umbilicus. On such occasions I have quite successfully used scissors. Always squeeze the blood supply up towards the puppy before you tear or cut.

Be sure to count placentas, for sometimes they are not automatically expelled with each puppy. You must be sure that your bitch has produced puppies and placentas in equal numbers for if retained the placenta can cause infection. Should you be short of one or more placentas tell your vet immediately and he will most probably give a pituitrin or similar injection to expel any waste matter safely. I prefer my own bitches never to eat more than one or perhaps two placentas for this will make their motions very loose, one problem a bitch and her owner can well do without.

It is not necessary to have all the puppies with the bitch throughout the whelping (they can stay safely in their nice warm box), although she will appreciate at least one when she is not one hundred per cent involved in producing the next whelp. I like to get the puppies on the teats as soon as possible and, concentrating on one or two puppies at a time, I find that in most cases they have all drunk by the time the last whelp has been produced.

Lhasa Apsos' litters vary in size and seem to be increasing as the years progress. Four or five now seem to be the most frequent number in a litter but there have been very occasional nines and I have heard of a litter of ten in the USA. The quietest and most contented litter I have ever bred was one of three – there was plenty of space, plenty of milk and a selection of teats always available – bliss, I suppose, if one is a tiny puppy!

After the whelping the bitch may have all her puppies put back with her but very shortly afterwards she should be taken out and given the opportunity to relieve herself. This must be closely supervised just in case there is another pup which has been tucked up behind the rib cage and which you knew nothing about! She will only wish to be away for a very brief moment so, rather than disturb her again, now is a good time to freshen her up a bit and make sure she feels comfortable before she returns to her babies. Do not keep her over-long but just wipe down her back end and dry it off as much as possible before putting her back. Be sure that she is offered plenty of glucose water but don't leave it in the whelping box, risking not only upset but danger to the tiny puppies.

By now you will hopefully have managed to weigh the puppies. Ideally it should have been done as the bitch was whelping for I think this helps you to keep an accurate picture in your mind of which pup is which. Be sure that you take descriptive notes on each puppy so that you can monitor progress without risk of confusion. Put down more than one distinguishing feature. '(1) gold bitch – 6 oz; (2) gold bitch – 7 oz' is simply not enough, for if the smaller gains weight more rapidly than the larger you will have lost check of them only too easily. I find

A contented litter of five healthy puppies with an equally contented dam.

it useful to mark down, for example, which feet, if any, are marked with white and whether perhaps there is a white flash on the chest. It is no good describing the puppies' features for they will change, but if there is any white on the coat it will stay for a little while at least.

Dew Claws

I also check for hind dew claws at the same time as I initially weigh the pups, and I make a note of these so that they are not missed when the vet comes to remove them. (Do not expect all or any of your puppies to have hind dew claws but some of them may; they should all have front ones.) When weighing I always keep to the same rota, taking the puppies in numerical order.

I have mixed feelings about whether or not dew claws should be removed. In a long-coated breed they can certainly get tangled in the coat or caught in play, but if one does not remove them one does prevent trauma to bitch and puppies in those early days. If they are to be removed this must be done at three days. The young puppies seem to forget their troubles very quickly; although, having said that, undoubtedly some vets are more adept than others!

If you do not wish to have the vet come to your home to remove dew claws you may take the puppies to the surgery but you will, of course, have to take 'mom' along too for she will be distressed if you all leave home without her. Take the precaution of waiting in the car until it is your turn to be seen, and the ever-loving mother will have to be kept well out of earshot when the vet is removing the claws for tiny puppies can make very large noises!

Determining the Colour Your Puppies Will Be

The genetic colour inheritance in Lhasa Apsos is both fascinating and complicated and for those who are interested in this aspect I have incorporated a short section concerning genetic colour inheritance in the very last chapter of this book. For the present, suffice it to say that though some, most or maybe all of your puppies will grow to resemble their sire or dam in colour, they can produce colours which are quite different. These are the result of recessive genes which express themselves just once in a while and take you almost completely by surprise.

The colour of young puppies will change, sometimes quite dramatically, as they grow, usually paling off to several shades lighter than the colour at birth. Usually a puppy will already have started to change colour by the time it leaves its breeder but its coat can go on changing well into adulthood. Indeed an Apso puppy registered as a gold sable can, by the age of about a year, have become almost silver sable, with just a slight golden hue in the sunlight. To get a fairly good indication of the final colour just peep under the tail: there is often a little patch of a quite different shade in that area and *this* is probably the colour the puppy will end up!

If you have bred a true black the skin will have a distinct bluish tinge to it. A puppy which looks black at birth but has a typical pinkish-coloured skin will dull down to a slate grey.

Our Standard, as we know, does not permit liver, but that is not to say that liver puppies are not born, for this colour, too, is carried as a recessive. At birth, livers have bright pink feet and their nose pigmentation is also pale; the coat colour is a sort of 'mushroom' shade. Liver puppies are, to the best of my knowledge, not culled as are undesirable colours in other breeds, and they make attractive pets. They cannot be shown, nor should they be bred from.

Weight Gain

As mentioned earlier, it is wise to weigh your puppies every day, at least for the first couple of weeks. You will find that they usually weigh between 5 and 8 ounces (140–225 g) at birth. As a very general guide you can expect each puppy to have doubled its birth-weight within the first ten days of its life. Some have doubled their weight at the close of the first week but they often slow down a little later on. A great deal depends on the size of the litter and how much milk the bitch is producing – and there is always one who seems to push everyone else off the very juiciest teat!

The following weight chart may be interesting for the sake of comparison. It shows increase in weight for a litter of four puppies born to a good brood bitch with an ample supply of milk. It may be interesting also to note the brief description I made concerning each puppy at birth.

1ST BORN – 9 pm – b. Black. Hind dew claws. Hind legs first.

2ND BORN – 10.05 pm – b. Gold with lighter feet. Hind dew claws. Head first.

3RD BORN – 10.50 pm – d. Black with slightly tan feet. Hind dew claws. Head first.

4TH BORN – 1.10 am! – d. Black with white front feet. Hind dew claws. Lodged sideways in canal, turned and assisted – finally, head first and still breathing!

DAY	DATE	WEIGHT	1ST BORN	2ND BORN	3RD BORN	4TH BORN
	Fri 7/10	at birth	$6\frac{3}{4}$ oz (190 g)	6 oz (170 g)	$5\frac{1}{2}$ oz (155 g)	$6\frac{3}{4}$ oz (190 g)
1	Sat 8/10	5.10 pm	7 oz (200 g)	$6\frac{3}{4}$ oz (190 g)	6 oz (170 g)	$7\frac{1}{2}$ oz (210 g)
2	Sun 9/10	10.00 pm	$8\frac{1}{2}$ oz (240 g)	$8\frac{1}{4}$ oz (235 g)	$7\frac{1}{4}$ oz (205 g)	$9\frac{1}{4}$ oz (260 g)
3	Mon 10/10	7.15 pm	$9\frac{1}{2}$ oz (270 g)	$9\frac{1}{2}$ oz (270 g)	$8\frac{1}{4}$ oz (235 g)	$10\frac{3}{4}$ oz (305 g)
4	Tue 11/10	9.15 pm	$10\frac{3}{4}$ oz (305 g)	11 oz (310 g)	$9\frac{3}{4}$ oz (275 g)	$12\frac{3}{4}$ oz (360 g)
5	Wed 12/10	11.30 pm	$12\frac{1}{4}$ oz (345 g)	$12\frac{1}{2}$ oz (355 g)	$10\frac{3}{4}$ oz (305 g)	$14\frac{1}{4}$ oz (400 g)
6	Thu 13/10	9.30 pm	13 oz (365 g)	$13\frac{1}{4}$ oz (375 g)	$11\frac{3}{4}$ oz (330 g)	$14\frac{3}{4}$ oz (420 g)
11	Tue 18/10	6.30 pm	1 lb $\frac{1}{2}$ oz (465 g)	1 lb 2 oz (510 g)	1 lb (450 g)	1 lb $3\frac{1}{2}$ oz (550 g)
15	Sat 22/10	9.30 am	1 lb $4\frac{3}{4}$ oz (590 g)	1 lb $7\frac{1}{2}$ oz (665 g)	1 lb $3\frac{1}{2}$ oz (550 g)	1 lb $7\frac{1}{2}$ oz (665 g)
17	Mon 24/10	8.30 am	1 lb $6\frac{1}{2}$ oz (635 g)	1 lb 9 oz (710 g)	1 lb 5 oz (595 g)	1 lb $9\frac{1}{4}$ oz (715 g)
18	Tue 25/10	11.00 am	1 lb $6\frac{3}{4}$ oz (645 g)	1 lb 10 oz (735 g)	1 lb 6 oz (625 g)	1 lb $9\frac{3}{4}$ oz (730 g)
22	Sat 29/10	1.00 pm	1 lb $9\frac{1}{2}$ oz (720 g)	1 lb $14\frac{1}{4}$ oz (855 g)	1 lb $8\frac{1}{2}$ oz (695 g)	1 lb $13\frac{1}{2}$ oz (835 g)

The above notes are exactly as I took them down (except for the metric conversions); had I felt that any puppy was gaining insufficient weight I would, of course, have weighed faithfully every day. As I was perfectly satisfied with their progress I weighed only on the days outlined above. My kitchen scales stop at 5 lbs (2.2 kg), but at eight weeks I recall that the big boy (4th born) went off the end of the scales, whilst the rest all weighed around $4\frac{1}{2}$ lbs (2 kg), give or take an ounce or two for 'wriggle allowance'.

Checking for Congenital and Hereditary Abnormalities

At birth the most important thing to check for is cleft palate, a defect in the roof of the mouth. It can usually be found by opening the puppy's mouth and checking with your little finger that the slightly ridge-like roof of the mouth is fully present. Should it be missing or impaired in any way your vet must be consulted immediately for, except in very minor cases which can sometimes be repaired with surgery, the puppy will need to be put to sleep as soon as possible for it will be unable to obtain nourishment. If cleft palate is repaired by surgery, under no circumstances should the dog in question be bred from or used at stud.

Any puppies in which a defective palate has not been detected at birth will usually show signs of the problem by lack of weight gain. Just occasionally the affected puppy may be able to suckle successfully but will be unable to take solids when weaning commences.

Hare lip is often associated with cleft palate and is more easily recognisable at birth. Again, minor cases may be surgically repaired but under no circumstances should such animals be bred from.

It goes without saying that any severely malformed puppies should be destroyed at birth. In such cases the reason for the deformity can indeed be genetic but it is also possible that the bitch may have had an undetected vaginal infection at the time of mating.

Blindness and deafness cannot possibly be observed until later, nor will you be able to detect the occasional defective coat pattern. I would draw your attention to the section concerning 'prapsos' which is included in the last chapter of this book.

WEANING

Provided that the bitch seems to be coping well enough and has plenty of milk you need not begin weaning the puppies until they are four weeks old. Puppies are especially susceptible to trauma at about three weeks so they should not be subjected to change unless it is necessary for the sake of the bitch.

I hesitate to give specific instructions as to how one should wean, for all breeders have their own personal preferences and indeed there are now some good specially prepared puppy feeds which seem to be used with success. Something which is common to all is that weaning is much easier if you begin when the puppies' tummies are empty rather than full. Try to time it so that you arrive with their food just as they awake from a nice long sleep. The ideal feeding bowl is one which is shallow but large enough for all the puppies to get their heads in so that they may feed together. Naturally, it will take the puppies a little time to adjust, but with patience and a sense of humour these early meal-times can be a great pleasure and after the first few days the puppies seem to know exactly what they are doing – which cannot always be said for their approach to the food bowl on day one!

The following weaning schedule is the one I normally follow and which seems to work well:

DAY 1 Introduce one milk feed around lunchtime. A rather 'sloppy' mix of Ready Brek or good quality oats with warm goat's milk and a teaspoonful of clear honey. (If you do not have a regular local supply of goat's milk which, by the way, freezes well, there are plenty of proprietary milk mixes designed specifically for puppies. What you must not do is change from one type of milk to another during the weaning process or you will have a number of upset tummies.)

DAY 2 Feed a milk meal, as above, at lunchtime and another milk meal (made up exactly the same) just before bedtime so that the puppies do not take too much from the bitch during the night.

DAY 3 Give the first milk feed first thing in the morning before the puppies have had time to feed off the bitch. At lunch-time introduce their first meat meal of well-soaked Vitalin (ideally put through a blender for the first few days) and Puppy Chum (very well mashed). Again feed a milk meal just before bedtime.

DAY 4/5 Breakfast and lunch as per day three. Then give a milk feed at tea-time and a meat meal last thing at night, thereby establishing a pattern of milk, meat, milk, meat.

It is not possible to be specific about how much to feed, for this will vary according to the number and size of the puppies and the bitch's milk supply. If you find that the puppies are not cleaning up their bowl completely and with relish, it is better to reduce the quantity of food given at each meal rather than leave out one of the scheduled feeds.

All this while the bitch should be spending longer and longer away from her puppies and the end of the weaning process seems to happen almost without noticing. The bitch will play her part in teaching the puppies to grow up and fend for themselves. I find that although she will usually continue to clean up after them when you start weaning, as soon as the meat feeds are introduced she will stop unless she is an exceptionally good brood. This is the 'messiest' time for any litter of puppies and you must endeavour to be scrupulously clean, changing newspaper and bedding as frequently as necessary.

You may find that you have to keep the bitch away from the puppies more than she wishes if her milk is not drying up as quickly as you would like, for there often seems to be one puppy which will cling to 'mom' as long as possible and, in doing so, he will encourage her milk supply to remain.

All the puppies should be completely weaned by about seven weeks so that they have been relatively 'independent' for a while before they leave for their new homes.

Notes on Puppy Care

UMBILICAL CORDS Check that the umbilical cords have dried up neatly. They will most probably have shrivelled and fallen off by the second or third day. If there is any sign of infection in the navel it should be bathed with antiseptic, and if it does not clear up quickly veterinary advice should be sought without delay.

UMBILICAL HERNIAS Umbilical hernias are found from time to time and these can in many cases be inherited. They can, however, also be traumatic, caused, for example, by an over-enthusiastic dam who has tugged too forcefully on the umbilical cord. When hernias are inherited I feel that breeders should make serious endeavours to breed them out. It is possible for a puppy not to have any problem with its hernia for the remainder of its life but there is always a danger of strangulation. My advice is always to let your vet have a look at any hernias your puppies may have so that he can recommend whether or not any rectification is necessary.

MUSCLE TWITCHING Ninety per cent of the new-born puppy's life will be spent sleeping and whilst asleep there will be a good deal of muscle twitching. This is perfectly normal and is an essential part in the development of the muscles.

NAILS Puppies' nails are sharp and can cause great discomfort to the bitch. It is a simple procedure to trim these with a pair of sharp, blunt-ended scissors on a regular basis.

DEHYDRATION Apso puppies should 'fill their skin' and if you can feel too much loose flesh, especially around the back of the neck, the puppy could well be dehydrating, which is cause for concern. If a puppy is limp when you pick it up there is clearly something wrong.

POOR SUCKERS Be sure that all puppies are actually drinking from the teats – sometimes they can be inclined to hang on to the teat without sucking. Constant crying of one particular puppy can often indicate that he is not getting all the milk he needs so put him on a nipple every two hours and check that he is swallowing, roughly at the rate of two swallows per second.

URINATION A crying puppy can also indicate that it needs to pass urine but that it has not been stimulated to do so, having been overlooked by the dam. You will find that you can begin to stimulate it yourself (see below) and then pass the puppy back to the bitch, rear end first, so that she may continue in her normal manner.

TOXIC MILK If any of the puppies seem to bloat, cry and have greenish-coloured diarrhoea with a red, swollen anus you must suspect toxic milk. Consult your vet immediately. You will probably find that the litter has to be hand-reared for infected milk could cause the puppies' early death.

STIMULATION If ever you have occasion to hand-rear a puppy do be sure to simulate the bitch's washing action after each feed (rub tummy and anus with a damp tissue). This will encourage the puppy to pass urine and defaecate.

EYES An Apso puppy's eyes will usually have opened between the ninth and eleventh day. When open, the eyes will be of a distinct bluish colour which will become darker later. They will not yet be able to focus properly and the puppies should be kept out of strong light. If any of the eyes are particularly sticky they may be bathed gently with a solution of warm, very weak tea but if there is any sign of infection contact your vet at the earliest opportunity.

EARS At birth the puppies' ears will be sealed; these will open usually between the thirteenth and seventeenth day.

SUCKING DUE TO TEETHING Apso puppies start teething at around three weeks, sometimes even earlier. It is especially at this time that they will try to suck on anything available, not necessarily a teat – it can be another puppy's leg, his ear or very often a little fellow's penis. The offenders must be discouraged from doing this.

SAFETY WHEN UP AND ABOUT The puppies should be able to get around on all four feet by about three weeks. At this stage be sure that they are safely enclosed for it is all too easy for them to escape and get stuck, lost and possibly hurt in places which are not intended for small puppies. It is not difficult to construct a play area which can be attached to the front of the whelping box for use when the puppies start to get around a little.

Care of the Bitch After Whelping and During Weaning

DISCHARGE After she has whelped the puppies a discharge from the vulva is quite normal. For the first couple of days this will be malodorous and dark in colour but should then change to blood red, later paling off to a mucous discharge. This discharge is caused by bleeding from the surface of the uterus where the placentas have broken away. If the thick discharge continues for more than a day or two seek veterinary advice without delay.

FEEDING The bitch's digestion will be a little delicate for the first couple of days after the puppies are born so she should be kept on a light diet of chicken or fish. In addition she will need plenty of fluids such as glucose water. I like also to offer a raw egg yolk (do not give raw egg white), mixed with just a little milk if she prefers it that way. The bitch may be so intent on her pups that she feels she has no time to eat, so if you have to coax her a little in the first few days do not be afraid to do so, even if it means hand-feeding. She will soon get back into her normal routine, and as the days progress after the litter has been whelped she will require more and more food, building up to twice her normal intake in the second week and three times as much in the third week, this being the period of heaviest lactation.

Keep to a number of small meals rather than occasional large ones, and your bitch may be grateful if you leave her something to nibble at during the night. Do not, of course, forget to leave water through the night, too. Whilst she is continuing to feed her litter keep up her intake of protein in relation to carbohydrates for protein helps greatly in the production of milk. As the puppies get closer to being fully weaned you can begin to cut down her intake of food again.

CALCIUM I mentioned earlier that calcium should be given but that opinions vary as to whether one should start giving it to the bitch whilst she is in whelp or after the puppies are born. I am now inclined to favour the latter for there seems to be fairly conclusive evidence that over-calcification of a bitch in whelp interferes with the body's calcium-regulating mechanism. If you decide to do the same be sure that your supply of calcium is at hand to be given from day one. It may be provided in tablet form or, better still, as a liquid, usually available from your vet. You must be sure that your bitch has taken the recommended dose (and remember that too much can be as bad as too little), so either give it to her 'neat' or, if she loves raw egg yolk as mine do, mix it in with that.

COAT CARE During the first couple of days she will not want to be messed with any more than is absolutely essential, but by day three she may be grateful for you to give her a little brush when you bring her back from one of her visits to the garden. Her coat will be very much out of condition whilst she is nursing the puppies and will mat more easily than you ever thought possible, so try to keep on top of the situation for the comfort of your bitch. Do not be surprised if the coat drops out; this does tend to happen in some bitches. If her long coat becomes too tangled there is also always a danger of the puppies getting entwined in the coat, which can have fatal results.

FAILURE TO CLEAN UP I have never yet come across a bitch who will not clean up scrupulously after her puppies but if she does seem disinclined a little smear of vegetable oil on the puppies may help her to get started.

OTHER PETS Whilst she is still feeding her puppies most bitches do not welcome other dogs in their presence. Other pets should therefore be kept out of the vicinity for the time being.

STRANGERS Under no circumstances should the bitch be disturbed by strangers during the first two weeks following the birth of her litter. Litters of new-born puppies are not on this earth to please the neighbours and all your children's schoolfriends. There will be plenty of time for the puppies to socialise later.

EXERCISE Make sure that the bitch gets sufficient exercise as she begins to leave the nest for longer periods. Do not, however, let her walk where other dogs may have been in case she picks up infection which can be passed on to her puppies.

REGURGITATION For a bitch to regurgitate food for her pups is perfectly natural as this would have been one of her methods of feeding in the wild. Whilst not a pretty sight, it will do no harm to either puppies or dam and you will find that the somewhat unsightly mass disappears quite quickly. It is sometimes said that a domestic dog will only do this if she is feeding puppies beyond the stage when her own milk supply will suffice, but I find that a very devoted Apso mother will regurgitate, often well after the puppies are fully weaned. In due course she will eventually give up this none-too-pleasant habit.

MASTITIS Keep a careful check on her teats to see that there is no sign of a mastitis developing. It will first be observed by one or more of the mammary glands becoming hot, hardened and inflamed. It will be sore for the bitch and she may well be distressed. If you catch mastitis in its very early stages you can try holding a warm cloth to the affected teats and endeavouring to express a little of the milk yourself. If milk can still be expressed, try then to encourage the puppies to use the affected ones. If hardening continues and the matter is not resolved within twelve hours seek veterinary advice immediately.

ECLAMPSIA Eclampsia is, in my opinion, one of the most frightening things that can happen to a bitch, the problem being that it can happen fast and the bitch can die within a matter of hours. Eclampsia, known in the human as 'milk fever', is caused not, as one might think, from a lack of calcium but by the body's inability to transport the calcium from the body reserves into the bloodstream.

The first outward symptoms can so easily go undetected: the bitch may appear a little strange and perhaps endeavour to make a nest, scratching up her bed just as she did shortly before whelping. She will probably seem restless and will pant more than usual, seeming at the same time 'edgy'. At this stage if you place your hands on her shoulders you will probably feel a slight tremble which will very soon become a shiver. Her legs will then stiffen and she will go 'wobbly', having difficulty in standing. As she worsens she will probably salivate and her pulse will become rapid. Eventually she will go into convulsions and her temperature will have risen to as much as 106°F (41°C).

Time is of the essence. The only way to save the bitch is by a massive calcium injection, which is usually given intravenously, although not always so. Veterinary help must be sought immediately and you must not be afraid to call the vet as soon as you realise what your bitch's problem might be, even though this may be in the middle of the night. When you tell him you think it is eclampsia he will, I assure you, understand completely. On the two occasions when I have experienced eclampsia I have given the bitch a good dose of liquid calcium as I have rushed out of the door on the way to the surgery (naturally telling the vet exactly how much I have given) – it may not have helped but I like to think perhaps it did.

You will have to take your vet's advice as to whether the bitch may continue to feed her puppies, although without doubt she will have to be taken away from them for a while. In serious cases some vets advocate taking her away from the puppies completely, for there is even greater danger to the bitch if she experiences eclampsia a second time whilst rearing the same litter. Even if you are told that the bitch may have her puppies back you should certainly work towards weaning them at an early age, even though she will most probably seem to have made a miraculous recovery. You will perhaps also wish to consider supplementing her feeds to take some of the pressure. Certainly it is most distressing for the bitch if she has to be taken away from the litter but, although I have not tried this myself, I believe it is possible to put her back with them if her teats are covered by something such as a large stretch stocking (making holes for the legs so that it doesn't slip). This will probably ease her mental anguish and she can continue to use her motherly instinct to wash her puppies.

METRITIS The first signs of a bitch having developed metritis are like to be a lack of interest in her puppies and lethargy. Metritis is an inflammation of the uterus and is caused by retention of a placenta or an unborn foetus. Here again you will recall how important it was to count the placentas and to consult your vet if in any doubt as to whether one or more may have been retained. Another reason for the development of metritis can be from bacteria introduced into the genital tract from, for example, unclean bedding or human fingers used as an aid to whelping. If caught in good time the problem can usually be rectified with a course of antibiotics, but severe cases, or those in which the bitch does not respond, are likely to necessitate spaying and can cause death.

If not treated in good time the bitch's milk will become toxic and the puppies will have to be hand-reared.

A Brief Word About Caesarean Section

Naturally it is your veterinary surgeon who must advise you on whether or not a Caesarean operation will be necessary to deliver the puppies. Thankfully the Lhasa Apso is not a breed in which 'Caesars' are common. If the reason for the Caesarean is one of inertia, either in its primary or secondary stages, you may find that the opinions of vets differ as to when the operation should be performed. Some vets like to operate if the bitch is three days overdue; others will wait for as long as a week. So much depends on the condition of the bitch and your vet will, of course, want to monitor the general activity of the puppies, checking, for example, that the heart-beats are still strong. It is at times like these that you will be glad that you have built up a rapport with your vet over the years and that you feel you can trust him implicitly.

Today there is relatively little risk to the bitch in a Caesarean operation, but none the less it should never be taken lightly as every operation carries with it a slight risk to the patient, and this is especially so if the bitch is already exhausted from her attempts to produce the puppies herself.

The usual reasons for a Caesarean operation are these:

- malpresentation – a puppy in a position in which it cannot pass normally through the birth canal. This may also block the way for the puppies which follow it and can cause danger to the dam.
- a particularly large puppy which the bitch cannot expel. This can sometimes be associated with a singleton (i.e. a litter of one puppy only), although to the best of my knowledge singletons are rare in the Lhasa Apso.
- uterine inertia – briefly, this is lack of visible contractions, even though other signs of the birth process are evident.
- a long and exhausting labour, in which the bitch may have produced some but not all of the puppies. Gradually she will have weakened to such an extent that the uterine and abdominal contractions have stopped.
- abnormal pelvic aperture due, for example, to a previous pelvic fracture or to a bitch with hindquarters constructed in such a way that the puppies will have difficulty in being passed normally. If you have any doubt as to your bitch's suitability for breeding make sure that she is checked over by your vet before she is mated, and especially if she has been involved in any road accident which may have injured her pelvis, even though there may no longer be any visible sign of a problem.

When you bring your bitch home from the surgery she will hopefully be fully alert and certainly her puppies should not be given to her unless she is. As she has not actually gone through the process of giving birth it may take her longer than usual to accept the puppies and for this reason you should begin by giving them to her one at a time. Try to get each one in turn to take some of her milk, for the colostral antibodies will only be present in her milk for the first twenty-four to forty-eight hours. Take special care of the bitch who has had her puppies by Caesarean, keeping a careful eye on her when she goes out to spend a penny just in case she pops any of her stitches. The way in which young puppies knead at the bitch's tender stomach will undoubtedly make you cringe, but most dams seem to tolerate their puppies' enthusiastic attentions and will usually treat them just as any other mother would once she realises that they actually belong to her.

If a bitch has had a litter by Caesarean section you will need to discuss with your vet the likely reason for the operation before you decide whether or not she should be bred from again. Depending upon the cause, a bitch can often have another litter quite normally but if she has a second Caesarean operation it would be most unwise to mate her again.

A Selection of Tibetan Names

The following Tibetan names may be of help when seeking names for new puppies. Some, you will notice, can be used for either sex and, strangely, I seem to have come across many more for males than for females:

116	MALE NAMES		
117	Ang Nyima	Jigme	Rinsing
118	Ang Pema	Kinthup	Semchumbi
119	Angtenjin	Konchhog	Shabdung
120	Ang Tharkay	Lhakpa	Sonam
121	Bom	Lobsang	Sunom
122	Da Namgyal	Mingma	Tensing
123	Dawa Thondup	Napboo	Tsereh
124	Dogomchen	Ngari	Wang Du
125	Dorjieff	Pemba	Wangyal
126	Gyamtso	Phudorje	Yuto

147	FEMALE NAMES		
148	Ang Lhamu	Pekyi	So-Nam
149	Chuni	Pema	Tashi
150	Daku	Pemba	Tsi Lhamo
151	Dekyi	Pem Pem	Yang Dra
152	Nima	Pur-Bu	
153	Norden	Rinzing	

10 Problems with Health and Ageing

Apsos are no more prone to illness than the majority of other breeds and indeed they encounter fewer problems than some for they are a relatively unexaggerated breed. But, naturally, even the most well-looked-after Apso can fall ill and if you are in any doubt as to the health of your dog your veterinary surgeon is the best person to give medical advice. The following brief summary of some of the problems one can encounter may, however, be of assistance, especially to the newer owner.

ABSCESS An abscess is very painful and under the Apso's profuse coat it is possible that it goes undetected until it has reached an advanced stage. It should be gently bathed in a solution of hot salt water which will bring it to a head and at which time it should burst so that the pus content is released and drained. Bathing should continue also after the abscess has burst for it must drain completely and therefore the skin must not be allowed to heal up too quickly. If the abscess does not burst or if more than one abscess appears you must consult your vet who, in any event, will probably recommend a course of antibiotics. Abscesses can appear almost anywhere and perhaps one of the most frequent reasons for their occurrence is following a quarrel with another dog, when the skin has been caught, albeit only slightly.

ALOPECIA Alopecia, or baldness, occurs when old hair drops out prematurely, the new hair not yet having grown in. This can quite frequently happen to a bitch which is rearing or has recently reared puppies and can also occur if an Apso has been given a course of cortisone or steroids. Should the cause not be known you must seek veterinary advice, for alopecia can be connected with a variety of disorders including hormonal imbalance and skin infections. Baldness in puppies is unusual but can cometimes be caused by a thyroid deficiency.

ANAL GLANDS If your Apso scoots along the ground on its backside it could well be that the anal glands are full and need evacuating. As discussed earlier, it is possible to evacuate the glands yourself but, unless experienced, I would suggest that you consult your veterinary surgeon for whom it is a very simple procedure.

CONSTIPATION Constipation can be caused by diet so you may effect a cure by altering your feeding programme. Try offering soaked biscuit meal rather than dry with any canned meats you feed and include some chopped green vegetables cooked in lightly salted water. As a temporary measure you might also offer a meal of uncooked red meat or liver, fed without biscuits. If you feed bones (which I personally do not recommend) there is a chance that pieces of chipped bone may have caused a blockage. Initially you can give your Apso a teaspoonful of olive oil which may ease the problem but if constipation persists consult your vet so that the cause may be determined.

COPROPHAGY (EATING OF FAECES) This most unpleasant habit usually manifests itself whilst still at the puppy stage, although occasionally a bitch can develop the habit after raising a litter. It is said that coprophagy offsets a lack of protein, vitamins or minerals in the diet but seemingly it can also come about in Apsos which are fed a perfectly balanced diet, leading one to suppose that in many cases it is simply a revolting idiosyncrasy! It has been said that adding a little fat or treacle to the diet helps but there seems to be no certain remedy, except to remove any excreta before the fellow with the nasty habit has a chance to get at it!

DANDRUFF If your Apso has dandruff or a dry skin it could be that he needs a little more fat in his diet. The problem may be rectified by mixing, for example, a little vegetable oil in each meal.

DEAFNESS As a congenital abnormality deafness seems to be rare in Apsos. However, full or partial deafness as a degeneration of old age can occur in any breed and is not always easy to assess. Deafness can best be tested by clapping your hands at a considerable distance from the dog to see if he responds. If you clap too close he may react to your movements or pick up the current of air which will give you a false impression of the severity of his impediment.

DIARRHOEA If your Apso not only has diarrhoea but also is obviously unwell, lacks appetite or has a tinge of blood in the motions, you must seek immediate veterinary advice. However, diarrhoea can also be caused by a slight chill or by a change of diet, in which case offer cooled, boiled water mixed with a little glucose powder and keep the dog on a light diet of fish or white meat for a while. Arrowroot can also usually be of assistance.

EAR INFECTIONS Because hair grows very deep inside the ear of the long-coated Apso, ear infections can set up very easily. For this reason always keep a careful check for any excess build-up of wax or ear mites, which can both give rise to canker. When grooming your dog you should automatically check the ear and if there is any sign of a foul-smelling discharge, possibly with an ear which is red and hot to the touch, you should seek veterinary advice immediately. Ear infections are painful and will almost certainly cause the dog to scratch the ear, thus increasing the irritation. A dog with an ear infection may also shake its head and hold the head on one side, usually with the affected ear downwards.

EYE DAMAGE Apsos' eyes do have a tendency to discharge a little but if they do so more than normally or if they are excessively watery, check to see that nothing is aggravating the eye. The long coat will, to a certain extent, protect the eye but a small piece of grit can become lodged or the eye can be scratched in a fight or in play. Simple cases usually respond to antibiotic treatment but prompt attention to eye injuries is important. If your vet prescribes an eye ointment hold the nozzle a little away from the eye and squeeze the ointment into the inner corner. Then close the eyelids together gently with your fingers to distribute the ointment over the eye.

FOREIGN BODIES LODGED IN THE MOUTH A dog which has difficulty closing its mouth, is constantly pawing at its mouth or is salivating heavily may have something wedged between its teeth or even across the roof of its mouth, between the upper molars. If you are unable to dislodge this yourself with relative ease, consult your vet straight away for, apart from the obvious discomfort to the dog, inflammation will almost certainly be caused.

FUR BALLS Because they are long-coated, Apsos are especially prone to fur balls, particularly so if they play with other long-coated dogs. I find that my Apsos will very occasionally vomit a fur ball without any fuss or bother and without previously having shown any sign of illness or discomfort. Fur balls, however, must never be regarded lightly as they can cause a dog to choke.

HARDERIAN GLANDS Some Apsos can have problems with the appearance of the harderian gland, which expresses itself as a 'lump' under the third eyelid, that is to say that you will see a red swelling in the inner corner of the eye. This is by no means common to all Apsos but it does crop up from time to time, usually in puppies between six weeks and six months old, although on rare occasions the harderian gland can appear in adulthood. If it appears on one eye it usually does so on the other, too, although not necessarily at the same time. Although the eye will look very sore (far more so than it actually is), do not be misled into thinking that it is a form of conjunctivitis. In the early stages you may find that the lump will come up and go down again but if it has once appeared, sooner or later it will be there to stay unless surgically removed or modified by inverting the gland back under the third eyelid. It is a simple operation for your vet to remove the gland and, once removed it will not re-appear. Some vets even carry out the operation under local anaesthetic. No stitches are usually necessary and the hair around the eye will not have to be clipped off. If your puppy has had to have a gland removed it will usually be fit and well enough to return to its usual routine or re-join its litter-mates within just a few hours. The harderian gland is, however, a source of tears which lubricate and moisturise the cornea, and if other lacrimal glands are damaged or if tear production declines with age there is a risk of 'dry eye' unless the gland has been modified rather than removed. Dry eye can usually be treated successfully if noticed in good time, so always keep a check on the eye for any alteration in its normal appearance.

HAY FEVER Dogs can have an allergy to pollens just as humans do and this will be displayed by excessive watering of the eyes and sneezing due to inflammation of the mucous membranes within the nose. Finding the best form of relief for your Apso is rarely easy but your vet, often by trial and error, can usually find something which will help to ease the problem.

HEART PROBLEMS It is rare to find a dog dying suddenly from a heart attack as we know it in humans, but dogs suffering from heart disease, especially when there is an obstruction in the flow of blood to the brain, do, indeed, collapse, becoming limp and unconscious. Frequently in such cases they recover within a matter of seconds when they need to be given fresh air. In coronary cases (i.e. poor blood supply to the heart muscle) the type of collapse is different in that the limbs usually remain stiff and the dog does not lose consciousness. The latter is not common in dogs but it goes without saying that in either case veterinary advice must be sought.

An older Apso may suffer from a weakening of the heart, indicated by a hard cough and lethargy, perhaps with breathing becoming more rapid than usual. If veterinary advice is sought in good time the problem may well be held at bay with a course of tablets and a controlled diet.

HEATSTROKE Extreme care must be taken not to leave Apsos where they will be exposed to excessive heat. It is surprising how quickly heat builds up in a so-called 'ventilated' car, even on a relatively mild day. To treat heatstroke, time is of the essence. The dog should be placed in the cool, and iced or very cold water should be liberally applied to head, neck and shoulders. If the dog is unconscious no attempt must be made to get him to take a drink but, once he has regained consciousness, and only then, he can be offered glucose water or a light saline solution.

INGUINAL HERNIA To the best of my knowledge such hernias, located in the groin area, are not especially prevalent in the breed. They can be found in both dogs and bitches and in one groin or in both, and sometimes they will not become apparent until the dog is well into adulthood. Veterinary advice should always be sought so as to determine whether or not surgical correction is necessary. It is undoubtedly unwise to use an Apso which has this problem for breeding purposes.

INTOLERANCE TO DAIRY PRODUCTS Whilst it is possible for some Apsos to be fed dairy products in moderation and without ill-effect, the majority of them do not easily tolerate such foods. If your Apso gets itchy or comes out in red patches or spots, especially on the tummy and under the legs, dairy products, or an excess of them, could be the cause.

KENNEL COUGH There are many different forms of kennel cough, all of which are highly contagious. The first sign of this viral infection is that the dog seems to be trying to 'clear his throat', and it is easy to think at first that he has something stuck. This uncomfortable noise gradually progresses to a hoarse cough. Veterinary treatment must be sought immediately, and for the sakes of the other dogs in the surgery, do not keep your dog with you in the waiting room. Kennel cough is highly infectious and your Apso must be isolated from all other dogs, not only whilst he is still 'coughing' but also for a good few weeks afterwards. Kennel cough can lead to bronchitis and is especially dangerous in young puppies, older dogs and those with a heart condition. Kennel cough vaccines are, however, now available.

KIDNEY FAILURE Primary signs of kidney failure are excessive thirst with the resultant frequent passing of water, accelerated breathing and premature ageing. Unfortunately kidney disorders do occasionally appear in young stock and it is possible that such problems in a youngster are inherited.

LAMENESS In an Apso one of the most likely causes of sudden lameness is that a clump of hair between the pads has gone unnoticed and has formed a hard ball which presses into the foot when the dog walks on it. In this case the tight knot must at all costs be very carefully removed with blunt-ended scissors (not an easy task, so do not allow it to happen in the first place!). A foreign object, such as a tiny stone, can also become wedged and can cause a dog to suddenly become lame. Check, too, that the lameness is not caused by over-long nails. Of course there can be many other, more complex, reasons for dogs becoming lame, so if the problem cannot be solved after careful inspection of the pads your vet should be consulted.

LIVER DISEASES All liver problems are serious so your vet should always be contacted at the very first sign of any disorder. A symptom which you will notice with relative ease is a jaundiced yellowing of the white of the eye and of the membranes lining the eye and the mouth. You may also notice a yellowing on the underside of the ear flap, less easy to detect in artificial light than in daylight. Other symptoms include sickness, loss of appetite, constipation and infrequent passing of highly coloured urine.

POISONING The initial signs of poisoning are various but can include sudden vomiting, muscular spasms and, in the case of Warfarin poisoning, bleeding from an exit point such as the gums. The antidote used will depend upon the type of poison taken – and remember that a dog can not only eat poison but can also walk on it and lick it from its pads. Seek veterinary treatment immediately and, if possible give the vet details of the type of poison with which you believe your dog has come into contact. When you telephone your vet take his advice as to whether vomiting should be induced for it is not recommended for all types of poisoning. Do, however, keep your Apso warm and quiet and let him have some fresh air.

THE 'PUFFS' There *may* be a technical name for this but if so I have never discovered it! It is not at all a major problem but it can be a frightening experience for the new Apso owner when it first happens. Caused by an elongation of the soft palate, and more likely to occur in the brachycephalic (short-nosed) breeds, the dog will suddenly draw in short, sharp breaths through the nostrils or mouth. When he does so he usually looks rather tense, standing four-square and with his head thrust forward. Again this does not happen in all Apsos but does seem to do so in a fair proportion, often especially when the dog becomes very excited. This 'puffing' will usually only last for a few seconds or perhaps a minute or so but you can stop it immediately by putting your fingers over his nostrils, thereby causing him to breathe only through the mouth – a quick and simple solution to this little problem. Of course there can, indeed, be other reasons for a dog puffing, such as, for example, a grass seed in the nasal cavity; naturally, should you suspect that the problem is anything more serious than the 'puffs' you must consult your vet.

SALIVARY FAILURE If an Apso is a poor eater it can, just occasionally, be due to the fact that he is not producing enough saliva. In the words of Lady Freda Valentine you should 'post a piece' – pop a small morsel of food into the mouth to help activate the salivary glands, thus stimulating the desire to eat.

SCRATCHING As mentioned earlier this can be due to a surfeit of dairy products but can, of course, be caused by a number of things. In a long-coated breed you must take special care that your Apso is not affected by fleas or other parasites. Bathing your dogs in an insecticidal shampoo should keep parasites at bay but other preparations can also be obtained, preferably from your vet. A dog which scratches behind its ear, often also making a rather vocal 'whining' noise, may well have an ear infection. Again, your vet should be consulted as to the most appropriate treatment.

SHEEP TICKS Sheep ticks can, unfortunately, be picked up not only from sheep themselves but also from the grass upon which they graze, so if you do walk your dog in sheep country be especially vigilant in checking his coat and skin on your return home. A sheep tick will, at first glance, look rather like a dark blue wart which will increase in size as the tick, whose head is embedded in the dog's skin, sucks on the blood. Ticks cause great irritation and your dog will probably let you know he has a problem by his constant scratching and nibbling at the affected area. The safest way to remove a tick is the application of salt on the tick but you must be sure that the head is fully removed or infection could cause an abscess to form. If you merely try to pull off the tick you stand a very good chance of removing the body without the head!

SNEEZING The cause of your dog sneezing must always be looked into urgently for it can be a sign of serious disease such as distemper. However, it can also signify that the membranes within the nose are inflamed, possibly due to an irritant such as a grass seed, perhaps a slight injury or even a parasite. Sneezing can also be the result of hay fever. If sneezing persists a vet must be consulted without delay.

SPINAL DISORDERS Because the Apso is a relatively low-legged, 'long' dog one must be on the alert for back problems, which seem to happen in the breed with more frequency than one would wish. Certain care should be taken, particularly with older dogs, when jumping on and off furniture. At any sign of spinal injury your vet must be consulted at once. Sometimes it is possible for the dog to recover, seemingly completely, but in other cases at least partial paralysis is the result.

STINGS Any dog which is stung in the mouth or on the throat should be attended to by a vet at once and an anti-histamine injection must be administered. Keep the dog cool and try to keep the tongue forward so that the airway remains clear. Perhaps the most usual place for a sting is in the pad of the foot and this is much less serious, though none the less painful. TCP will usually bring some relief and vinegar is particularly good for wasp stings. Bicarbonate of soda can be applied to bee stings when the sting has been removed with tweezers.

TOOTH PROBLEMS Lhasa Apsos are prone to losing their incisor teeth sooner than dogs with a longer foreface and scissor bite. It is also likely that those puppies which develop their teeth later than the majority have a tendency to lose them sooner, possibly because the teeth are more shallowly rooted. Often a tooth can be lost without any apparent distress to the dog and without the owner even noticing until grooming up for the next show! To help avoid decay, the teeth should be kept free from tartar. If you are not proficient in keeping your dog's teeth tartar-free yourself, your vet will usually be quite willing to carry out a scale and polish. A dog which is suffering from toothache will usually rub its head constantly along the ground and may be reluctant to eat; some swelling may also be noticed.

TRAVEL-SICKNESS Many Apsos never suffer from travel-sickness at all; others, unfortunately, do. Usually you will know when your Apso is a puppy whether or not he will suffer in this way and often he will overcome the problem as he matures. Travel-sickness can display itself simply as excessive dribbling, or a dog can throw up all the way to a show! Mercifully there are now some extremely good canine travel-sickness tablets on the market, available from good pet stores or from stalls at dog shows.

UMBILICAL HERNIAS See Chapter 9, concerning whelping and weaning. Just occasionally a rather different type of hernia, also located in the umbilical area, can present itself much later in the life of a bitch which has undergone a Caesarean operation. This is a result of an adhesion on the scar tissue and medical advice must be sought as to whether or not removal is necessary.

UNDESCENDED TESTICLES A male Apso in which neither testicle is descended is known as a cryptorchid; if only one is descended he is a unilateral-cryptorchid. Technically the common term 'monorchid' should be applied to dogs which only possess one testicle. In the Apso the testicles have usually descended fully by the age of six months and often very much sooner. In the majority of cases cryptorchidism (and monorchidism) is hereditary and breeding from such stock is definitely not to be recommended; such a dog may, however, be capable of reproducing. Veterinary advice should, in any event, be sought for there is a risk of a tumour forming in a testicle which is retained.

VOMITING An Apso may vomit a clear, white or yellowish bile from time to time, usually due to a mild gastric irritation or indigestion. It can be helpful to 'starve' the dog for twenty-four hours, offering just cooled, boiled water with a little glucose powder added. Constant vomiting of any kind or vomiting with evidence that your Apso other-wise feels unwell is cause for a visit to the vet.

Care of the Elderly Apso

A Lhasa Apso often lives for a good few years more than many breeds of dog and, without doubt, if you care for your canine companions you will wish to give them every comfort they deserve in their closing years. Be sure that they have adequate warmth, high-quality food and that they are exercised sensibly. If you normally feed only one meal daily you would be well advised to split this into two smaller meals which not only aids digestion but also gives another 'highlight' to the day. Do not allow an 'oldie' to become overweight, remembering that older dogs have a tendency to put on weight more easily than youngsters. Excess weight will put undue pressure on the heart and this is often detected by an unpleasant cough. Weight can, of course, also have an adverse effect on various other organs and on the limbs.

A cough can, of course, also be a sign of worms and it is wise to keep all your dogs wormed regularly, the older ones on an annual basis. If, however, your older dog is in ill-health do take your vet's advice before worming.

Do not subject the older dog to over-long grooming sessions but keep them regular and fairly short. Make every effort to avoid letting him get damp or cold and, when bathed, make sure that he is kept in a pleasantly warm temperature for a good while afterwards.

If teeth have been lost or have loosened, take more than usual care as to the consistency of the foods he is given but do not deprive him of all his much-loved chewy things. It is surprising how an Apso without any incisors left in his head can thoroughly enjoy a good chew with his back teeth! Just use your common sense and avoid, especially in his regular meals, anything which he seems unable to manage. For example, it may be a good idea to use a puppy meal instead of the slightly larger biscuit meal you usually feed and if you feed proprietary tinned dog food (one of the better quality ones of course), you may consider serving the puppy variety which will be of a more manageable consistency. Naturally, if your dog has a medical condition which requires a special diet your veterinary surgeon will advise what is best, often recommending one of the high-quality low-protein diets now available.

If his sight is failing avoid moving the furniture and certainly his own 'personal items' more than is necessary. In this way he will be able to get used to exactly where things are so that he still feels fairly confident, mishaps and accidents being kept to a minimum.

Talking of mishaps and accidents, an ageing dog can sometimes have difficulty in controlling his 'water-works'. This can be for a variety of reasons and undoubtedly if this problem occurs you should consult your vet to determine the cause. Do not scold the older dog severely for accidents of this nature, for there will almost certainly be a medical reason for a generally 'clean' dog disgracing himself. It would be wise always to put down a thick wad of newspaper in the hope that he will use this if you are not going to be around to let him out when nature calls. If your vet asks for a urine sample for analysis, try to obtain the first urine of the day. Do not spend hours trying to get the dog (who, by the way, thinks you have gone quite mad!) to aim straight into the little sterilised bottle you intend to give to the vet, but catch the all-important urine in a sterilised, stainless-steel container and then pour this into the bottle – you will find this much easier, I assure you!

I would normally advise that a young puppy should not be introduced to live with an older dog, and certainly whether or not this should even be considered is very much dependent upon the personality of the older dog, his ailments and one's own domestic circumstances.

Undoubtedly a youngster must only be kept with him under constant supervision and the old gent must have plenty of time to himself so that he can take thorough rest when needed. In my own case I did allow an old man to live, for a few hours a day, with a youngster. I felt that it might give him added interest for he was doing little more than sleeping and could no longer manage proper walks. The enjoyment he derived from the youngster's company in those last few months of his life was immeasurable. He played like a puppy, only for moments at a time, but one could see how he looked forward to his new companion's visit and I feel sure it gave him something interesting to dream about in those many hours of sleep.

Naturally, if one does keep young and old dogs together one has to be ultra-cautious for the sake of both puppy and older dog, special care being taken that the old chap does not snap and injure the youngster. Most important of all is never to let the older dog feel that he has been pushed out to make way for the youngsters; he must be made to feel just as important as he has always been and, what is more, he needs to have that little extra attention to make him feel even more special. As in all aspects of kennel management, so much comes down to pure, basic, common sense.

Time To Part

Sooner or later the dreaded time comes around. If you are lucky your old dog will die peacefully in his sleep without pain, sparing you the anguish of wondering whether or not the time has come to take the decision of putting him out of any misery he may be suffering. Thankfully vets are able to prescribe some excellent pain-killing drugs so that in many cases a dog can have a major and terminal illness without suffering pain. But when the pain-killers no longer have sufficient effect, or if your dog is no longer able to live in comfort and with dignity, the time has come to part.

Having a dog put to sleep brings with it inevitable distress to the owner, but do try not to show the dog how upset you are; there will be plenty of time for tears after he has gone. If possible choose a vet with whom both you and the dog are familiar. The vet will usually visit your home if you wish, or alternatively you can take your Apso along to the surgery. If your dog has established a friendly rapport with your vet over the years he will probably go into the surgery expecting his usual routine check. If he is in pain he will very possibly associate the surgery with the place to which he goes when he is in pain, after which that pain is relieved. And this is just the way it will be. If you feel you can keep control of your emotions in front of your beloved pet, stay with him whilst he is injected so that he has your reassurance as he goes finally to sleep. That sleep comes quickly and almost imperceptibly. He has given you many long years of faithful service – try not to let him down at the last.

After he has gone the vet will take charge of the disposal of the body if you wish or, provided that there is no serious risk of infection, you may have him back to bury, perhaps under his favourite tree. There are, by the way, some special metal trunks available for the purpose should you so wish.

Those who wish neither to leave their dog with the vet nor to have him buried in the garden can take advantage of one of the commercial pet cemeteries, details of which are usually available from your vet. The vet can often arrange for your dog to be collected and taken to the 'cemetery' where he can be either cremated or buried. The ashes can be scattered in the cemetery gardens and a plaque can be erected or a shrub planted in your dog's memory. Alternatively you may have the ashes returned to you. Naturally there is a fairly substantial charge for this service but most also offer the option of having one's pet cremated with others in order to keep costs to a minimum.

Whilst on the unhappy but inevitable subject of parting, owners might also like to consider making some provision for their Apsos should they themselves depart this world first. When making out your will speak to your solicitor about how the dogs can be included. In doing so you will feel comfortable in your own mind that the Apsos who have shared your hearth will be taken care of in the manner you feel will be best for them. After all, they are your dogs; you have lived with them for many years; you and your Apsos will almost certainly have learned to know each other very well indeed.

11 Further Notes on Breeding and Genetics

This closing chapter of the book will, hopefully, be of interest to those who wish to delve more deeply into some of the more intriguing aspects of breeding Lhasa Apsos.

'Prapsos'

A 'prapso' (sometimes known as 'perhapso') closely resembles a Tibetan Spaniel in appearance but it is *not* a Spaniel: it is a smooth- or short-coated Lhasa Apso which is produced as a result of mating Apso to Apso.

Prapsos, it seems, can be produced in a variety of colours, and it is unlikely that any colour is exempt from the possibility of carrying the genes which produce the short coat, although the coat texture tends to vary according to the colour produced. Test matings can, however, help breeders to establish which dogs carry the genes and which do not.

One or more prapsos can be born in a litter and the other members of that litter can be perfectly normal-looking, long-coated Lhasa Apsos. In general the outward appearance of a prapso is that the feet and forelegs are smooth, with some feathering between elbow and ankle and between the toes. There is feathering on the hindquarters down to the hock and the tail is well plumed. There is, however, a lack of head furnishings and no heavy feathering on the ears, whilst the body coat can be short and smooth or fairly short and rather harsh to the touch, somewhat as if the coat has been broken off at the ends. In the latter case there is usually a smooth patch below the eyes and it is most often the golds and shades of fawn which have the silkier coats. The feet of a prapso are rather fine and narrow, again much more like the hare foot of the Tibetan Spaniel.

Recognition of a prapso in the nest is not usually possible before the age of about four weeks, by which time it most probably has a full set of teeth and is more active and noisier than its litter mates. The pattern of coat development will appear much as it is on the rest of the litter until around seven weeks of age when the hair on the muzzle seems to disappear, in addition to which the breeder may notice that the puppy looks finer in bone and that the bones of the feet are slightly elongated.

There are some puppies which do not display all the characteristics of a prapso but, none the less, in maturity have a very short coat (perhaps only 4 inches/10 cm) and of a harsh texture; the above signs may or may not be evident until much later. This makes for added confusion if, by chance, one is sold with papers before the problem has been detected. It goes without saying that when this defective coat pattern is discovered the dog should be eliminated from any future breeding programmes. The greatest danger, of course, arises if the puppy has been sold to a pet owner who has no regular contact with Lhasa Apso breeders and is therefore unaware that there is a genetic defect, assuming merely that they have an Apso with a shorter coat than expected. If the dog is retained merely as a pet that is fine, but if the novice owner breeds from the bitch the problem is exacerbated. Perhaps a word of caution is due here to owners of stud dogs, who should most certainly refuse to allow their dogs to be used on prapso bitches or those with a short, harsh coat which is clearly uncharacteristic – one assumes, of course, that owners of dogs which are at public stud are knowledgeable enough to differentiate between an Apso with a defective coat and one which as been clipped down in a puppy trim!

In the various test matings that have been carried out over the years, smooth to smooth seems to produce an all smooth litter; smooth to long coat produces predominantly long coats, with the odd smooth; and long coat to long coat can produce all long but sometimes the occasional smooth. Thelma Morgan worked out some ratios in about 1960 and came to the conclusion that around six per cent of Apsos were born with smooth coats. Prapsos are still produced but unfortunately they are often 'swept under the carpet' making it difficult to calculate any accurate or even representative figures and, of course, there are now many more breeders than there were in 1960, making the task virtually impossible.

One must never lose sight of the fact that long-coated Apsos which are litter mates of a prapso may indeed be carriers of the smooth factor and yet this may not be expressed for many generations. If we are to hope to eradicate or reduce the overall number of prapsos they must not be sold with papers and should not be bred from unless for the specific purpose of controlled test matings in order to establish which dogs in one's own breeding programme are carriers of the smooth factor. This is something which should only be done by the most dedicated and experienced breeders and only for the purposes of research and eradication, *not* just to produce a litter of interesting puppies!

It certainly seems that prapsos are the results of 'throw-backs' from generations past and one is tempted to think of Dr Greig's theory that the Lhasa Apso is the result, over four centuries ago, of a cross between the Tibetan Terrier and the Tibetan Spaniel. The very nature of this book (the purpose of which is to help rather than to confuse) prevents me from going into great depth, but suffice it to say that genetic experimentation regarding a number of factors (not just smooth and long coats) in other breeds proves that if prapsos were the result simply of a cross between the two breeds then we should have been able to breed it out to a much greater extent many, many generations ago. The problem is of a very complex nature in that the smooth factor is displayed so very infrequently and in such an irregular pattern. Indeed it is possible to breed for many generations without ever producing a prapso and then, quite unexpectedly, one will appear and take you completely by surprise.

If you do come across a prapso (or semi-prapso) in one of your litters you will assist the development of the breed if you talk about it rather than conceal the fact, for only by bringing problems such as these into the open can we hope to make strides ahead in the future.

Genetic Colour Inheritance

The coat colours of Lhasa Apsos are thoroughly fascinating and, almost certainly, more complex in their make-up than almost any other breed. One could study colour inheritance for a lifetime and I believe that in the Lhasa Apso one would still have the occasional surprise. I do not wish to suggest, however, that the few pages which follow cover all the combinations of colour, nor do I necessarily believe that future research will not bring to light other factors which may have a bearing on my findings thus far.

Sadly, due to its very complexity in this breed, colour genetics take so very much time to analyse but I thought that this section may just stimulate some breeders to look more closely into the reasons behind the colours in the Apso and it will, I hope, serve as a foundation and stimulus for those who may wish in the future to research the subject further. What you read here is the result of research which I carried out a few years ago. I very much hope that one day I shall have the time to develop it further myself.

Coat colours principally found in the breed: black; black and white particolour; slate; silver sable; silver; silver and white particolour; dark brindle; red gold; gold sable; gold; gold and white particolour; pale gold; and white. Liver is also found, affecting both coat colouring and skin pigmentation.

As will be appreciated each 'colour' has a multitude of different varieties and no two Apsos seem to be of quite the same 'shade'. A colour with white is not always a particolour but may be, for example, a black with white markings. One can also have a combination such as black with tan markings, although I suspect the genetic make-up of what we call 'tan' to be that of gold sable or gold, depending upon the depth of colour involved. Added to this, a dog's coat colour frequently actually changes visibly in a matter of months, in which case it often also changes back again to its original colour! In other cases the colour changes with maturity, but even though the change may be quite dramatic, if one searches beneath the coat one can usually find a trace of the original hue.

Some of the combinations I have observed and on which I based my original research were the following:

black × silver sable	has produced	black
black × dark brindle	has produced	black
		+ gold sable
black × gold sable	has produced	liver
		+ silver sable
		+ black
		+ gold sable
		+ gold and white
		particolour
black × slate	has produced	black
slate × gold	has produced	dark brindle
slate × silver sable	has produced	gold
		+ gold sable
slate × black	has produced	black
silver sable ×		
gold and white		
particolour	has produced	gold sable
silver sable × black	has produced	black
silver sable × gold	has produced	gold sable
silver sable × gold sable	has produced	silver sable
		+ gold
silver sable × slate	has produced	gold
		+ gold sable
silver × gold	has produced	gold
		+ silver sable
		+ slate

dark brindle × black	has produced	black + gold sable
dark brindle × gold	has produced	gold sable + dark brindle
gold sable × gold	has produced	gold sable
gold sable × gold sable	has produced	gold + gold sable
gold sable × silver sable	has produced	silver sable + gold
gold sable × black	has produced	liver + silver sable + black + gold sable + gold and white particolour

gold sable ×
    gold and white
    particolour
	has produced	gold sable

gold × slate	has produced	dark brindle
gold × gold sable	has produced	gold sable
gold × silver sable	has produced	gold sable
gold × dark brindle	has produced	gold sable + dark brindle
gold × gold and white particolour	has produced	gold sable + gold
gold × silver	has produced	gold + slate + silver sable

**gold and white
    particolour** ×
    silver sable
	has produced	gold sable

gold and white particolour × gold	has produced	gold sable + gold
gold and white particolour × gold sable	has produced	gold sable

The above combinations are only a very few but, used purely as an example, one can observe the following:

(a)   That of five different colours crossed with silver sable only one has produced a silver sable puppy. Thus perhaps silver sable is the result of a recessive gene.

(b)   That of five different colours crossed with gold sable three have produced gold sable puppies – more than fifty per cent, therefore this could perhaps be a dominant colour.

(c)   Of six colours crossed with gold only one produced gold but four produced gold sable. Is this another indication that gold sable is dominant? Likewise perhaps gold is recessive.

(d)   Three gold and white particolours were crossed with other colours. None produced a particolour but all three produced gold sables. Perhaps further proof of the deductions made in (b) and (c)?

(e)   Slate was crossed with three other colours, none of which was gold sable. However, no slate puppies were produced but one gold sable puppy was.

(f)   Black is supposedly dominant in canine coat colour genetics but it is rumoured that in Apsos this is not so. Of four blacks crossed with other colours, all of these combinations have produced black. This leads me to suppose that the rumour is incorrect and that black is indeed dominant.

Thus, with a very limited amount of personal research, one can deduce that:

  – black is dominant   – slate is recessive
  – gold sable is dominant   – gold is recessive
  – silver sable is recessive

Here I would ask readers to note that I am fully aware that research behind other lines may, indeed, produce other theories but, as I said before, I believe that these findings are highly relevant for those wishing to carry out research of their own.

Based on the above information I believe that a gold sable dog can be denoted as 'e^{br}', and that a gold dog can be called 'e'.

If one takes the mating of two gold sable parents which produced two gold and three gold sable puppies one can deduce that both parents were heterozygous for gold sable (thus '$e^{br}\, e$'), for 'e^{br}' is epistatic to 'e'. That is to say that 'e^{br}' conceals 'e'.

| | | *Sire* | |
		e^{br}	e
	e^{br}	$e^{br}\, e^{br}$ (gold sable)	$e^{br}\, e$ (gold sable)
Dam			
	e	$e^{br}\, e$ (gold sable)	$e\quad e$ (gold)

Had both parents been homozygous 'e^{br}' no gold puppies would have been produced:

	Sire	
	e^{br}	e^{br}
e^{br}	e^{br} e^{br} (gold sable)	e^{br} e^{br} (gold sable)
e^{br}	e^{br} e^{br} (gold sable)	e^{br} e^{br} (gold sable)

(Dam on left)

Likewise no gold puppies would have been produced if one parent had been 'e^{br} e' and the other homozygous for 'e^{br}'; this, again, being due to the fact that 'e^{br}' is epistatic to 'e':

	Sire	
	e^{br}	e
e^{br}	e^{br} e^{br} (gold sable)	e^{br} e (gold sable)
e^{br}	e^{br} e^{br} (gold sable)	e^{br} e (gold sable)

(Dam on left)

However, if one looks further back in the ancestry of this same litter the facts become increasingly complicated, for neither of the parents (both gold sable) has gold sable parentage themselves. One generation further back, however, one finds at least one gold sable.

In the previous generation gold sable appears again and the chart opposite shows a most intriguing picture:

My own personal research becomes more and more complex and would undoubtedly be of interest to a very small proportion of readers so I shall just give my findings of one particular exercise for your reference.

Assume that four separate matings are made, each one being a solid gold to a gold sable and white particolour. Each 'pair', however, although outwardly alike, has a different genetic make-up to produce the phenotype (outward appearance). Assuming that four puppies are born in each litter, the most likely results of these hypothetical matings are thus:

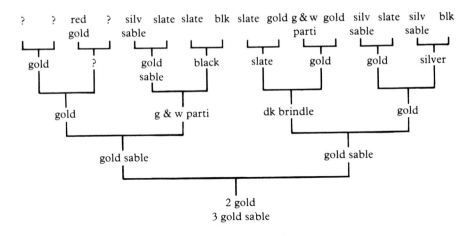

MATING A   All four puppies are gold sable.

MATING B   Two puppies are gold sable and two solid gold.

MATING C   Two puppies are gold sable and two are gold sable and white particolours.

MATING D   One puppy is solid gold, one gold sable, one gold and white particolour and one gold sable and white particolour.

It is interesting to note that no particolours are produced in the first two matings outlined above, but in the following generation, if one were to carry out a litter brother to litter sister mating, there would be a twenty-five per cent chance of producing one. We can also see that in mating A not one of the four puppies would resemble its sire or dam in colour. Thus we can see how easy it is for colours to 'get lost' and to reappear in future generations.

Suffice it to say that the subject is thoroughly absorbing and that those whose appetite has been whetted will probably take up pedigrees, pens and papers and start working on colour analyses this very minute. I fully appreciate that others will quite definitely not! None the less, whether one's interest lies in genetics or aesthetics (or both), I feel sure you will agree that the very splendid array of Apso colours enhances the charm of the breed.

INBREEDING, LINEBREEDING AND OUTCROSSING

We mentioned earlier that there are three forms of breeding, inbreeding, linebreeding and outcrossing. Inbreeding is when one mates together a dog and bitch of very close parentage, such as father to daughter, mother to son or brother to sister. Half-brother to half-sister matings are also often classified as inbreeding, though others might consider this linebreeding. Often the closeness of the matings behind the sire and dam will tighten the lines even more, so it is highly relevant not only to look at the prospective puppies' immediate ancestors but also to look a number of generations back. It is possible to work out percentages so that one can see exactly how much influence any given dog is likely to have on the resultant offspring.

Inbreeding is likely to show up both the good and bad points of the stock used and is not for the faint-hearted, for if anything unpleasant is hidden away now is the time that it is likely to show up. Undoubtedly inbreeding is, however, one of the most effective ways of fixing type. Such close breeding is not something which can be done for generation after generation. It is generally used only by the experienced breeder who in a well-planned breeding programme will probably only inbreed closely once in a while, the rest of the time using linebreeding with the occasional outcross.

The following examples show very close breeding and are all based on matings which have actually taken place.

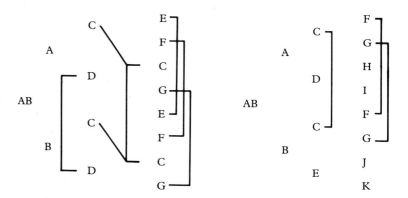

The diagram (left) represents a full brother to full sister mating, which in itself is very close. The closeness of the mating is amplified by the fact that 'C' is also the father of 'D', thus the previous generation was also inbred (father/daughter). As a result this three-generation pedigree shows only seven ancestors out of a possible fourteen.

The diagram (right) is a straightforward case of a half-brother to half-sister mating, with no additional relationships to complicate the issue. It is the least close form of inbreeding with eleven ancestors shown out of a possible fourteen.

Linebreeding is less close but still involves breeding to dogs which are related. Theories vary, but provided that common ancestors appear within the first four generations of a pedigree the offspring are said to be linebred. If the link-up is further back than that, many would call this outcrossing. Linebreeding is undoubtedly the most usual form of breeding in Lhasa Apsos but if it is used as a sole method of breeding it can bring with it problems. Although most breeders use linebreeding as their primary method of breeding it is usually combined with occasional outcrossing or inbreeding. The ways of outcrossing are numerous and the following are just a few examples:

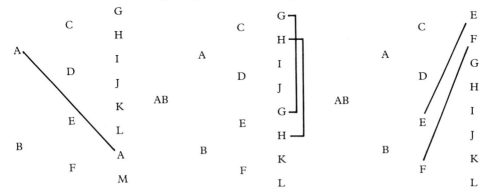

The diagram (left) is an example of a simple grand-sire to grand-daughter mating and features thirteen different ancestors in the three generation pedigree. Clearly the offspring are likely to derive the greatest contribution from ancestor 'A'.

The middle diagram shows a clear case of linebreeding with two common ancestors in the third generation. It is a cousin to cousin mating for, as we see, 'C' and 'E' are full brothers. Thus the offspring have twelve different ancestors in the first three generations.

In the pedigree shown right we see how ancestors 'E' and 'F' both play an equal part in contributing a proportion of their genes to the litter born. 'E' and 'F' are both grand-parents and great grand-parents.

Lastly, let us look at a linebred pedigree in which a grand-sire, technically, has as much genetic influence on the offspring as do the sire or the dam. I have shown percentages and we see that the sire and dam each provide fifty per cent, the grand-parents twenty-five per cent each and the great grand-parents twelve and a half per cent each. (See p. 160).

The reason for the strength of influence from this grand-parent is that he was also the great grand-sire on two counts so, in effect, he will have passed on fifty per cent of his genes to 'AB'.

It goes without saying that in linebreeding one should always aim to 'double up' on dogs which possess features which you desire, for we

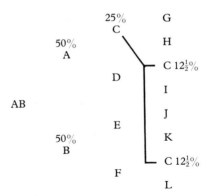

have shown, especially in the last example, how a dog to which one has linebred can have a great influence on the puppies one hopes to produce.

An example of outcrossing is clearly not necessary for every ancestor in the first three generations (at least) will be different. When one does choose to outcross it is often done with the aim of bringing into one's breeding programme a feature which needs developing or amplifying. Selection of a stud dog for an outcross mating will, of necessity, have to be made on the phenotype of the dog but a careful breeder will also carefully observe his offspring so that one can have a fair idea of what he is producing when mated to other bitches.

Postscript

And so we must come to the close. If this book has helped just a few Lhasa Apsos to live better lives, or to be better understood by their owners, then it has served its purpose. If its readers have derived just a fraction of the pleasure and interest that I have experienced in my research and writing, then the rewards are twofold.

Appendix 1 Useful Addresses

THE KENNEL CLUB
1–5 Clarges Street
London
W1Y 8AB

THE LHASA APSO CLUB
Miss J. Cunliffe
Hon. Secretary
Lundy Cottage
Painscastle
Builth Wells
Powys LD2 3JJ

MIDLAND LHASA APSO ASSOCIATION
Mr T. Richardson
Hon. Secretary
89 Belt Road
Hednesford
Staffordshire WS12 4JJ

SOUTH EAST LHASA APSO SOCIETY
Mr R. Witham
Hon. Secretary
Clovelly Cottage
Bournebridge Lane
Stapleford Abbots
Romford
Essex RM4 1LU

THE TIBET SOCIETY
Olympia Bridge Quay
70 Russell Road
London
W14 8YL

THE TIBET FOUNDATION
43 New Oxford Street
London
WC1A 1BH

(Current details of breed club secretaries can always be obtained from the Kennel Club)

Appendix 2 Registration Numbers in the UK – a significant selection

1935 – 10 registrations
1936 – 25 registrations
1937 – 21 registrations
1938 – 16 registrations
1956 – 21 registrations

1984 – 1304 registrations
1985 – 1404 registrations
1986 – 1487 registrations
1987 – 1447 registrations
1988 – 1503 registrations

References

1   *Indian Kennel Gazette* – December 1957. (article by Mukhandi Lal)
2   J. Taring – *The Tibet Journal*. A highly respected Tibetan, for eighteen years
    Mr Taring served as a high-ranking government official in Lhasa and following
    his exile became Director of Tibetan Education until his retirement in 1975.
3   'A brief account of Tibetan dogs' – delivered by Mr Lhalungpa, 1970.
4   *Dog World Annual* 1929.
5   *Dog Owners' Annual* – Lionel Jacobs, 1901.
6   *Our Dogs* – Christmas, November 1949.
7   *Kennel Gazette,* April 1934 – notes on Tibetan dogs by Hon. Mrs Bailey.
8   *Dog World*, 2nd March 1940 – 'These breeds must not be allowed to disappear'
    by Thelma Gray.
9   *Dog World* – 8th February 1952 – 'Tibetan breeds' by Audrey Ferris.
10 *The Cassell's Book of the Dog* (1907) by Robert Leighton.
11 *The Twentieth-century Dog* (1904) by Herbert Compton.
12 *Our Dogs* – August 1929 – Mr Hally's column.

Selected Bibliography

Books

ASH, E. C., *Dogs and Their History,* Vol. 2, Ernest Benn, 1927.

AVEDON, JOHN, *In Exile From the Land of Snows,* Wisdom Publications, 1985.

BAILEY, LT-COL. F. M., *No Passport to Tibet,* Rupert Hart-Davis, 1957.

BELL, SIR CHARLES, *Portrait of the Dalai Lama,* Collins, 1946.

BUCKLEY and STRAUSS, MICHAEL and ROBERT, *Tibet – A Travel Survival Kit,* Lonely Planet Publications, 1986.

BYLANDT, COUNT H. DE, *Dogs of All Nations,* Kegan Paul & Co., 1904.

CARMELLO and BATTAGLIA, DR and L., *Dog Genetics – How to Breed Better Dogs,* TFH Publications Inc., 1978.

COLLIER, V. W. F., *Dogs of Japan in Nature and in Art,* William Heinemann, 1921.

COMPTON, HERBERT, *The Twentieth-century Dog* (Non-Sporting Vol.), Grant Richards, 1904.

CROXTON SMITH, A., *About Our Dogs, The Breeds and Their Management* (2nd edition), Ward Lock & Co. Ltd, 1951.

CROXTON SMITH, A., *Dogs Since 1900, Non-Sporting Breeds – Some Far Eastern Dogs,* Andrew Dakers, 1950.

CUTTING, SUYDAM, *The Fire Ox and Other Years,* Charles Scribner's Sons, 1940.

DADDS, AUDREY, *The Shih Tzu,* Popular Dogs Publishing Co. Ltd, 1974.

DAVID-NEEL, ALEXANDRA, *With Mystics and Magicians in Tibet,* Penguin Books, 1931.

DUNCAN, RONALD CARDEW, *Tomu From Tibet and Other Dog Stories,* Methuen & Co., 1950.

EASTON and MCDONALD BREARLEY, REV. D. ALLAN and JOAN, *This is the Shih Tzu,* TFH Publications.

FRANKLING, ELEANOR (Revised by Trevor Turner, BVetMed, MRCVS), *Practical Dog Breeding and Genetics,* Popular Dogs, 1981.

GELDER, STUART and ROMA, *The Timely Rain,* Hutchinson & Co. Ltd, 1964.

HADFIELD, CHARLES and JILL, *A Winter in Tibet,* Impact Books, 1988.

HARRER, HEINRICH, *Seven Years in Tibet,* Rupert Hart-Davis, 1955.

HARRER, HEINRICH, *Return To Tibet,* Pinguin-Verlag, 1983.

HERBEL, NORMAN and CAROLYN, *The Complete Lhasa Apso,* Howell Book House Inc., 1979.

HUBBARD, CLIFFORD L. B., *Dogs in Britain,* Macmillan & Co. Ltd, 1948.

HUTCHINSON, W. (Ed), *Hutchinson's Popular Illustrated Dog Encyclopaedia,* 1933–1934.

JOHNSON, NORMAN H., *The Complete Book of Dogs,* Robert Hale & Co., 1965.

LANDESMAN and BERMAN, BILL and KATHLEEN, *How to Care for Your Older Dog,* English Library, 1980.

LEGL-JACOBSSON, ELIZABETH, *East Asiatic Breeds*, Tryck Produktion, Sweden, 1978.

LEIGHTON, ROBERT, *The New Book of The Dog*, Cassell & Co., 1907.

LEIGHTON, ROBERT, *The Complete Book of The Dog*, Cassell and Co. Ltd, 1922.

LHALUNGPA, MR, *A Brief Account of Tibetan Dogs*, The Apso Committee, New Delhi, 1970.

LITTLE, CLARENCE C., ScD, *The Inheritance of Coat Colour in Dogs*, Howell Book House, 1979.

MCDONALD BREARLEY, JOAN, *This is the Lhasa Apso*, THF Publications, 1977.

MARPLES, THEO, *Show Dogs – Their Points and Characteristics*, Our Dogs, 1920.

MIGOT, ANDRE, *Tibetan Marches*, Rupert Hart-Davis, 1955.

NIBLOCK, MARGARET, *The Afghan Hound, A Definitive Study*, K & R Books Ltd, 1980.

RICHARDS, DR HERBERT, *Dog Breeding For Professionals*, THF Publications, 1978.

SEFTON, FRANCES, *The Lhasa Apso*, Frances Sefton, 1970.

SHAW, VERO, *The Encyclopaedia of The Kennel*, George Routledge and Sons Ltd, 1913.

SIMSOVA, SYLVIA, *Tibetan and Related Dog Breeds, A Guide to Their History*, Tibetan Terrier Association, 1979.

SOMAN, MAJOR W. V., *The Indian Dog*, Popular Prakashan, 1963.

THOMAS, LOWELL JR, *Out of This World*, Greystone Press, 1950.

ULLMAN, JAMES RAMSEY, *Man of Everest, The Autobiography of Tenzing*, George Harrap & Co. Ltd, 1955.

VESEY-FITZGERALD, BRIAN, *The Domestic Dog*, Routledge & Kegan Paul Ltd, 1957.

WATSON, JAMES, *The Dog Book* (Vol. 2), Doubleday Page & Co., 1906.

WEST, GEOFFREY, MRCVS, *All about Your Dog's Health*, Pelham Books, 1979.

WEST, STANLEY, *The Book of Dogs*, Alexander Ousley Ltd, 1935.

WHITE, KAY, *Dogs, Their Mating Whelping and Weaning*, K & R Books Ltd, 1977.

WHITE, ROBERT C., MRCVS, *Sewell's Dog's Medical Dictionary*, Routledge & Kegan Paul, 1976.

WOODHOUSE, BARBARA, *The A to Z of Dogs and Puppies*, Barbara Woodhouse, 1971.

WYNYARD, ANN LINDSAY, *Dog Directory Guide to Owning a Tibetan Spaniel*, The Dog Directory, 1980.

WYNYARD, ANN LINDSAY, *Dogs of Tibet and the History of the Tibetan Spaniel*, Book World, Rugby, 1982.

YOUATT, WILLIAM, *The Dog*, Longman, Brown, Green and Longmans, 1851.

YOUNGHUSBAND, SIR FRANCIS, *The Epic of Mount Everest*, Edward Arnold & Co., 1926.

Newspapers and Periodicals

So many articles have been used as sources of reference that it is simply not feasible to list all the particular issues in which they appear. However, the following publications are of great interest:

LHASA APSO CLUB (UK) – handbooks, booklets and newsletters.
MIDLAND LHASA APSO ASSOCIATION (UK) – newsletters.
CLUB DES CHIENS DU TIBET (FRANCE) – newsletters.
The Lhasa Apso Reporter (USA).
Dog World – newspapers and annuals.

Our Dogs – newspapers and annuals (Will Hally's 'Foreign Dog Fancies' in
    newspapers from the early part of this century give an enormous amount of
    information concerning the breed).
Kennel Gazette – of special interest are the issues of December 1901 and April 1934.
Country Life – issue of 18th January 1962.
The Complete Dog – published monthly in 1972 by Peter Way Ltd.

Other publications which are of particular interest have been listed as source material.

Most interesting articles concerning Tibet and the surrounding regions are to be
found in the *National Geographic Magazines* of: July–December 1928 pp 569–619,
July 1931, October 1935, June 1944, May 1949, May 1951, March 1952, December
1952, July 1953, July 1955, October 1962, March 1963, October 1966, October 1974,
November 1976, April 1977, March 1978, February 1980, February 1982, June 1982
and March 1984; also in the *Geographical Magazines* of: October 1946, December
1947, October 1956, September 1960 and April 1961; and in *Living Races of Mankind*,
Vol. VI, published by Hutchinson.

Index